Reading to Our Children

An Act of Love

Mary Kretlow

Reading to Our Children: An Act of Love
by
Mary Kretlow

Published by: Nicasio Press
                California, USA

ISBN: 979-8-9864100-8-1

Dedication

To the readers and listeners who, through the power and joy of a story, will make the world a better place.

ACKNOWLEDGEMENTS

Without the support and experiences of my family, friends, and literary advisors, this book would still look like a cookbook full of ideas. Thank you to Jeanette Taylor who kindly told me to rewrite the cookbook and cautioned me that this might be a long process.

Thank you to all the courageous and honest parents, grandparents, teachers, and caregivers who shared their stories with me. Your love for your children came through in every interview. I am much obliged to: Kate, Chris, Anna, Luci, Katie, Catherine, Marjorie, Emily, Kienna, Mary M, Gretel, Brant, Brenda, Selma, Regina, and Pauline.

A special thank you to Gretel, whose words helped to inspire the title for this book.

Thank you to fellow writers Patricia Boham and Marion Waters. Patricia made sure I was at my desk and chatted with me every week about my progress. Marion and I frequently compared notes and talked about the publishing process. You both were pillars of support.

Thank you to my editor, Laura, whose patience and expertise enabled me to get this book to publication. Your assistance was invaluable.

Finally, a really big thank you to all my family who always shared their enthusiasm and support for this book. For my daughter, Emily, who is such a blessing, I thank you for your insight into schools today and your artistic flair. For my husband, Don, I am forever grateful for your keen eye for details. You are my constant companion to share my ideas.

I hope that the love, kindness, and knowledge that was shared with me can now be passed on to other families as they become read-aloud advocates.

CONTENTS

Reading to Our Children

An Act of Love

READING TO OUR CHILDREN

INTRODUCTION

Quiet, peaceful, nap time at our house was often followed by a storm. When Emily would get up, this normally happy, bubbly little girl was grumpy—I mean really grumpy. She would not want to talk or engage in any activity or play with friends. And sometimes it went from bad to worse and then she would just be a mess, in tears and very distraught. I had to find a solution. Then I thought, if books calm her at night before she goes to bed, why not try books after a nap? So, when she started to stir from her nap, I quietly and without a word picked her up and moved to the big comfy rocker and just started reading. For two or three books, there was no chit chat, no discussing pictures, no interactions. I just quietly read, turned the pages, then picked another book. Gradually, Emily would start to point at something on the page or utter a few words, and soon we would be fully engaged with her books. The grumpies were gone, and life would resume. This became a routine following her afternoon nap, a time to slowly re-engage with the world on her own terms.

As a parent, I used reading aloud to calm, educate, nurture, inform, and entertain our daughter. My husband or I read aloud to Emily every day from the time she was an infant until she was about twelve. For the most part I loved it, but I have to admit there were times I was so tired, so busy, or so overwhelmed that the thought of reading one more book was just too much. My husband read to Emily as well, and together we had created this granite-like routine that Emily looked forward to and would not even contemplate sacrificing. Try as we might to sometimes fake it, we would invariably be caught out. My husband sometimes fell asleep mid-sentence, and I could hear Emily prodding, "Daaaaad, wake up!" Or he would be so dog-tired, making up his own story, weaving in and out of comprehension that Emily would get really frustrated, and again I would hear, "Daaaaad, that's not how it goes." My approach when I really wasn't into it would be to ruthlessly abbreviate the text, ("Mom!!!! you forgot to read it all!"), pick really short books, or speed read…none of which would be acceptable according to Emily's standards. But we persevered, and the rewards were remarkable.

Remarkable, because it wasn't just about telling stories. It wasn't just about reading or preparing her for learning. Emily could depend on a daily time with Mom or Dad. This helped to create our strong emotional connection and was a time to discuss important issues that might arise through the story. It was fun. It was important. And because it was so routine and dependable, it was also a time when events of the day or questions might be discussed.

When Emily was a toddler, she liked the lessons of the *Berenstein Bears* books and would often comment on how it related to her own life. The first novel we read was *Fantastic Mr. Fox*, a delightful, fast-paced adventure story about a family of foxes. The author, Roald Dahl, is a favourite with children, and this particular novel had plenty of dialogue, so four-year-old Emily was really engaged. We shared many wonderful picture books and novels, and now that Emily is an adult, we still talk books and share our favourites.

One of the main keys to unlocking this treasure is to make it enjoyable, engaging, and anticipated. We want our children to eventually do this activity joyfully on their own and later, pass it on to their children. I am not suggesting that reading to children is the only path to success and happiness, but it is just so darn powerful.

Before I knew about the power of a story as a parent, I had explored the significance of the read-aloud as a teacher. I knew children loved stories and I was curious about those children who didn't seem to have this experience. While it was no surprise that children arrive at school with all kinds of differences, abilities, and experiences, they all seemed to arrive hopeful. The smell of new books and crayons accompanied each excited and sometimes anxious child. Most children understand that school is a place where they will learn new things. In fact, whenever I asked a child why their parents sent them to school, the answer was always the same: "To learn."

As those first few days passed, it soon became obvious that some of the children had not experienced the joy and richness of a regular story time. They had trouble sitting and listening, stories did not seem to hold their attention, and they were starting to lose their initial excitement about school. They were already behind their peers. Children who start behind often stay behind. This thing called "school" did not seem fun; it was hard and unrelenting. Imagine what that does to a child's self-esteem. Teachers will adapt their programs to meet the needs of the child but they cannot magically make all children catch up or duplicate what could have happened between birth and kindergarten. I say this not to blame parents as many do the absolute best they can and many face challenges that are overwhelming. Parenting today is not the same as parenting twenty, thirty, or forty years ago.

Benefits of Reading Aloud

Does reading to your children really make a difference? Absolutely. As a teacher, I had the skill to impart information on how to read, but I could never replace a caregiver's influence from birth to five, and that window is a critical time for optimal child development. Parents and caregivers can lay the foundation for positive academic, physical, and social well-being that will help to give their children the best life possible. Continuing to read with your child after age five will give you the opportunity to keep lines of communication open and is an avenue to explore deep questions, wonders, problems, and world issues.

Reading to a child will reap lifelong cognitive and emotional benefits. I am not talking about actually teaching your child to read. Just read aloud every day. It takes a commitment, but it is an opportunity too precious to waste. In fact, I am so convinced of the power of reading aloud that I feel it should be placed right next to food, water, and air in our hierarchy of needs. Reading aloud *is* connection—it is love, and it is learning.

There are many situations that make it difficult, if not downright impossible, to make reading with your child an everyday practice. If you do not have basic needs like shelter, food, and physical safety adequately met or if you are in a traumatic situation, sick, or suffering from abuse, reading with your children may not hit your radar. We must have compassion for parents who are in these situations and do all we can to advocate and support them and their children.

What's in This Book?

If you are ready and able, this book will give you the confidence and tools to make reading aloud to your children a daily habit. Although reading aloud is best started when your child is an infant, you will learn all is not lost if you start later. You will learn about the positive achievements your child and you will gain. You will learn practical ideas, how-to suggestions, and advice about managing the technology giant that lurks in our homes. You will learn where to find books, how to work with the wiggly child, and some great book suggestions. And last, but not least, you will learn to become a beacon for the family read-aloud and you will want to empower others, because we all want a better world for our children.

So, let's get started; there's no time to waste. A thousand stories wait to be told and your child is eagerly waiting to hear them.

Author's Note

In this book, when I refer to family, parent, or caregiver, I mean all possible configurations—whoever is entrusted to care for a child. I also refer to mothers, fathers, grandparents, siblings, and other caregivers when the distinction is important.

Anecdotes in this book are in italics, and the initials or name at the end of the anecdote indicate the source. The anecdotes were drawn from interviews and conversations with parents and caregivers of young children, used with permission.

Compelling Reasons to Read Aloud

Life is busy. Parenting is hectic. Work is demanding. Where do I get books? How do I fit in reading aloud to my child? It seems like a frill and a chore. Isn't reading something I should leave up to teachers? Is it really all that necessary?

I am here to convince you that reading is not a frill, it is not a distasteful chore, and today, more than ever, it is an activity that can connect you to your children in a positive, fun, and forever kind of way. After interviewing many parents, I realized most read to their children for a couple of reasons: for fun and getting a jumpstart on learning to read. While these are really important reasons, there are more. I learned from parents and teachers how, especially after the global pandemic, our children are needing our attention, love, and guidance more than ever. Parents also expressed concerns about excessive use of devices that have become too prevalent as babysitters, entertainers, and teachers.

Reading aloud to your child is not a frill, and the benefits will outweigh any doubts you may have. What you first considered a chore may in fact be a pleasure. Reading aloud to children isn't just about the skill of reading. This book will explore five major areas of benefit to you and your child. Just this one activity, done regularly from birth, affirms that reading aloud is:

- A time for fun
- A time for calm
- A time for seriously connecting with our children
- A time for preparation for academic success
- A time for adults to benefit

If you didn't start reading to your child the minute they popped into this world, don't worry—you can still make a huge impact by starting now. Whether your child is two or seven or even nine, reading aloud will make a difference.

A Time for Fun

> *When I say to a parent, "read to a child," I don't want it to sound like medicine. I want it to sound like chocolate.*
>
> Mem Fox

Let me tell you a story from my own experience: In a small, four-room country school in a remote logging community, my Grade One students were going to the library for the first time that year. One child in particular stood out. Shane was a sweet child who was popular and fun to be around. He had an elfish quality about him and could light up a room with his presence. He loved to tell jokes and make his friends laugh. Going to the library was a big deal. Our small community did not have a public library, so the school was the only source for children's books. Most of these children had experienced the pleasure of signing out one book a week in kindergarten, but now they were in Grade One, and they could sign out two books. Two books that you could actually put in your backpack and take home for a whole week.

As the librarian was showing us around and pointing out the books she thought the children would enjoy, she casually indicated the bin with the joke and riddle books. Shane's eyes lit up and he quickly chose the books he wanted: *The Funniest Joke Book Ever* and *Silly Jokes for Kids*. He renewed those books over and over, and soon every staff member knew what Shane had clutched tightly in his little hand as he roamed the school seeking willing "victims" for his jokes.

"Do you want to hear a joke?" he would ask. Then he would painstakingly sound out the words:

"W..wh..wh..a..t...what...is...bl..bla...blac..k... black...a.n.d...and..w...h..wh..i..whi..t..whit ...e ... white..and..r..e...d..red..a..ll..all...o..v..ov.e..r...over? What is black and white and red all over?"

The listener would patiently say, "I don't know. What is black and white and red all over?"

"A... new...news...pa..pap...er...A NEWSPAPER!"

Shane would chuckle like it was the funniest thing ever. Then he would look up at you and say, "Wanna hear another one?" His motivation to decode those squiggles on the page was making people laugh, and he was having a good time. And along with this fun came his improved ability to read. He was one of the first children in the class to succeed in blending words and understanding text. And he did it because it was fun and he loved it.

Fun is serious business in a child's world. So often we marginalize fun and miss the real impact this provides in our lives. *Fun* is a word children understand as something they like to do and want to do again and again. Play is how they learn. For adults, the word *fun* often implies pleasure, amusement, or simplicity. No hassles, no strife, lighthearted. Not every reading time will be a rip-roaring laugh-fest, but some will be and some will just fall in that category of pleasurable.

If we want to sustain reading over a lifetime, it must be pleasurable and for children, it must be seen as fun.

Oh, and don't claim reading books is fun if your child doesn't agree with you. You will need to figure out what would make it fun. Is your session too long? Are you insisting on stillness? Are you choosing all the books? Are you asking too many questions? Have you just taken away the smartphone and insisted that books are better? (Your child won't think so.)

Catherine Price, author of *The Power of Fun*, offers this definition:

> True Fun…is the feeling of being fully present and engaged, free from self-criticism and judgement. It is the thrill of losing ourselves in what we're doing and

not caring about the outcome. It is laughter. It is playful rebellion. It is euphoric connection. It is the bliss that comes from letting go. When we are truly having fun, we are not lonely. We are not anxious or stressed. We are not consumed by self-doubt or existential malaise. There is a reason that our moments of True Fun stand out in our memories: True Fun makes us feel alive.

She goes on to say in her book that you don't always have to have all three—playfulness, connection, and flow —to have fun. Just one of these will make a fun time. Two or three of these criteria mean more fun.

Imagine giving yourself over to this state of fun every day. You will find that these enjoyable, fun sessions with your child will actually destress you and give you more energy for all the other must-dos in your life.

A favourite story time in our family was just before bedtime. Freshly bathed and in soft warm pajamas, Emily would eagerly climb into bed, position her favourite stuffies, and await the final closure to her day. The first thing she would ask for was to be told all the "fun stuff" she did that day. Having me recall the details of the day gave her another opportunity to relive the fun—a little like watching a video or telling a story called "Emily's Day." She would get a dreamy look and occasionally comment when I recalled the positive aspects of her day. Her definition of fun was anything that was perceived as "nice," "good," or "exciting."

I knew exactly what she wanted to hear and recounting these activities for her was like writing a gratitude journal for me. To see the good through the eyes of a child is very rewarding and reminded me that it's really the simple little pleasures of life that make us happy. We would talk about making pancakes with Daddy, swimming in the icy water at the beach, using the new feather duster to help Mommy with the chores, singing "Monkeys on the Bed" while jumping on the couch, or playing with Rachel and making surprise snacks. I would end with, "And now you are tucked into bed waiting to hear a story." Emily would choose a book, and even though I might be bone-tired, I felt good as a parent and happy that Emily thought her life was fun.

Children like to laugh, play, and learn. They are naturally curious and seek out fun. The language of early picture books is often full of rhyme and nonsense words. The pictures are mini-works of art and are often comical. Children delight in trying out the different words or acting out the pictures on the page. It is a time to let imaginations go wild, find the inner child in yourself, and for a small space of time, let go of the heavy concerns of daily life and just play. Sharing these delights with your child will help to cement the bond between you, and perhaps pave the way for a lifetime of sharing pleasurable activities.

Older children will find their own niche for what books bring them pleasure, but it has been my experience that some children will revel in potty humour, or gross or icky things well through the primary grades. Joke books are another source of amusement. Some children find their fun through how-to books that teach them cooking, constructing, collecting, gardening, or playing an instrument. Other children love to immerse themselves in the predictable comfort of a series and enjoy visiting the same characters time and time again. Sometimes it is a genre, like fantasy or adventure that will become a favourite. Maybe your child will gravitate to non-fiction because dinosaurs or airplanes or science is so interesting. Learning, as Albert Einstein says, is "when you are doing something with so much enjoyment that you don't notice that the time passes." Think carefully about the likes and passions of your child and find books to match.

The Importance of Self-Selection

Perceiving that books and reading are fun requires children to be able to choose the books they like. Self-selection begins with the books in your home. Although you or another adult has bought these books, it is important to let your child make the choice from among those books. When you visit a library or bookstore, make sure your child has the opportunity to select the books they want. If their choices are boring to you or you just can't face reading *Green Eggs and Ham* one more time, try introducing new material or having a "Mommy's choice." Self-selecting books however, should be the bulk of your child's reading material. It validates a child's preferences and identity.

> **Children are more likely to read, read more, and enjoy books whey they make their own choices.**

They may not choose the books we like because they are their own little beings with likes and dislikes that are unique to them. Honor their choices. Older children may bring home books you do not think are appropriate. This is an opportunity for a conversation. Ask them questions like, "Do you understand what is happening in this book?" "What appeals to you about this book?" "Is there anything that makes you uncomfortable in this book?" Calmly tell your child why you object to a book and listen objectively.

from BRANT:

Wrenlee likes to choose her own books and even though she is not even two, I would say she likes to be in control of her books.

A Word of Caution

Don't try to push ideas, teach literacy, or enforce stillness when reading to your children. The more you push, the more they will resist being read to and associate reading with something that is to be avoided. Remember, you want reading to be a pleasure your child will choose for the rest of their lives, so keep it fun, read the books they like, and make this a time that is much anticipated.

I recall a parent who lamented the fact that her son liked to read what she considered junk. Joey wanted to read comics and sports books, but his mother had other ideas about the material he "should" be reading. She always chose the books from the library, books that were "quality" literature and would read aloud books she thought he should hear. Although Joey was an early reader, he never chose what his mother wanted him to read. She said he would hide his comics or sports books under the mother-approved text and find ways to read only what he wanted. I encouraged this mom to let Joey read the books he preferred and perhaps negotiate a book to read aloud. Children's book choices will change throughout their childhood, and it is important to be respectful of their preferences.

Sometimes it will take a little effort to make or keep your reading sessions fun. Below are four suggestions that may ramp up the reading pleasure.

Types of Books for Fun

So often we get stuck reading the same book or types of books over and over so try something different. Poems are often overlooked so introduce your child to authors like Jack Prelutsky [JP], Dennis Lee [DL] or Shel Silverstein [SS]. The humour will hook your child.

> When Tillie ate the chilli
> She erupted from her seat
> She gulped a quart of water
> And fled screaming down the street...JP

> Alligator pie, alligator pie
> If I don't get some I think I gonna die
> Give away the green grass, give away the sky
> But don't give away my alligator pie...DL

I made myself a snowball
As perfect as could be
I thought I'd keep it as a pet
And let it sleep with me…SS

Humour is not only in poems. Try books like *Elephant and Piggy* or *Scaredy Squirrel*. The Humour section at the end of this book will give you more suggestions. Another idea is to have a "baby book" time with your child. Choose old favourites and have a trip down memory lane at the same time. Finally, share an online book together. The important word in that last sentence is *together* because an online book by itself can be just bells and whistles. I will write more about this later in the book.

New Voices

Children love to hear you read but what about Grandma or Grandpa? An older sibling or other relative? Your child will benefit from the diversity of reading styles and also give them opportunities to bond and make positive connections with other members of your family. Even if other family members are not available, you can switch up your reading voice. Try singing a short book or reading the whole thing in a baby voice or deep voice. Your child will love the variation.

New Places

Bedtime is always a favourite time and place to read to children, but there are many other options. Make a tent in the living room, get a flashlight, and read books while "camping." The car is a great place to tell stories or listen to an audio book. Visit some places that you have read about like a park, the ocean, construction sites, or a swimming pool. Take advantage of free story times a libraries, schools, or community events.

Activities

Another way to enhance fun is to extend the ideas presented in stories by making food that was read about, drawing like the illustrator, or dressing up like one of the characters. Give your child a gift card for a bookstore and plan a shopping trip together. Invite your child to include all their stuffies or pets as guests during the next read aloud. If your child likes to craft, find a book and try creating some of the suggestions together.

Sometimes fun just happens. While you are reading, you or your child may come up with a great idea for an extension of the book. Just go with it and enjoy the results.

Reflect to Remember: A Time For Fun

- Children are programmed for fun and play. It's how they learn.
- Self-selection is important
- Try new ideas to ramp up the reading pleasure: new voices, new places, new activities

---

A Time for Calm

Reading forces you to be quiet in a world
that no longer makes place for that.

John Green

I recall one Christmas when we had many family members for dinner. Following the meal, the children were a little aimless, so they began to bug each other and then started to wrestle. They were having fun but we could all see it start to escalate and warnings from their parents were not heeded. I grabbed a book and started to read out loud. Soon all three children were standing around my chair as I held the book so all could see, their eyes glued to the page as they searched for the hidden objects in the picture. My voice was calm, and I made eye contact with each child as they carefully scanned the page. Interestingly, it wasn't only the children that were engaged with the book. Every adult in the room was also listening to the story. We should never underestimate how telling a story can be captivating and pleasurable …and calming.

When the books come out and your child knows its story time, it's like they enter a different world. Disconnecting from our busy, hectic life can be a challenge. If your child is really hyper or distraught, you can use reading to restore calm. Sometimes it helps if you have a space with fluffy pillows or a favourite blanket, but just the sound of your voice reading a story will draw your child into another world anywhere and at any time.

If you are trying to calm a child, don't choose a rollicking, noisy adventure story. Choose a book carefully, one that tells a gentle story. Is this a *Goodnight Moon* time or *Don't Let the Pigeon Drive the Bus* time? Adjust your voice by reading slowly, quietly, and with conviction. Take long, deep breathes, exhale without hurrying, and soon your child will be drawn into the lovely pictures and a story world's away from where they were ten minutes ago. As your voice becomes quieter and slower, you may find that your child will begin to mirror your behaviour.

Children's books that teach about mindfulness—an ability to pay attention to what's going on inside ourselves and to live in the moment—may also be good choices. These books talk about breathing techniques, quiet places, rest, and calm.

Books about nature can also bring calm—not books about tornados or earthquakes but books about the forest, a nature walk, the seashore, or the first snow. These are books of wonder as well as calm. Maybe your child has a particular enveloping interest. An interest that pulls them into another world, enough to calm and satisfy.

Gradually, you will notice your child can sit and listen for longer and longer periods. This is excellent preparation for the classroom, eating in a restaurant, sitting through a church service, visiting the doctor, or spending time on individual pursuits. Reading books can also be a self-regulating activity. Self-regulation is a term used to describe a state wherein we can adjust our emotions and behaviour. It is an ability to calm oneself and focus. It is wonderful to see young children start self-regulating by choosing a book and "reading" on their own. If you have used reading aloud to calm your child, have a short conversation later about how reading calmed them down and how that felt.

from KRISTA:

My husband and I took our three kids to a family event at the community centre. One of the activities was the story lady. She was dressed in colourful clothes and was a magnet of interest for young children. My kids, ages 2, 4, and 6, sat down on her carpet and joined several other children. The story lady began to read a rather long story, and slowly many of the kids lost interest and wandered away. I looked at my kids, each hanging on every word and just mesmerized by the story.

By the end of the book, my children were the only ones left. They have been read to since birth and they know the joy and the power of a story and even the two-year-old can sit and listen for ten minutes. I was so thankful that I read to my kids every day and they can be calm and happy listening to a story.

Just imagine your child being calmed by a book. You no longer hear a loud boisterous child. The book has drawn them into another world. Why not go there every day in the company of your child? Why not look forward to it?

Later we'll discuss, in detail, how reading aloud is beneficial for adults as well. Don't deny this little beam of joy and delight that is waiting for you every day.

Alternative Methods to Sitting and Listening

What about all those wiggly children for whom *calm* might have an alternate meaning? Sitting for long periods of time is not normal for really young children, and they biologically need to move, as it is important for brain development and physical health. Some children just need to always move something! Wherever you are in your read-aloud journey, realize it is a process, and each child responds differently. Here are three creative ways to read to a wiggly child.

1. Choose a place where is child is already "captive." Read during mealtimes, at bedtime, in the bathtub, or while playing with toys or colouring. In the car, try an audio book or make up a story.
2. Choose your book carefully. It should be of high interest and not too lengthy. Maybe you only read one or two pages. Choose a book that invites finger play or other actions. Stories that invite sounds (animal sounds, machine sounds) will also engage a wiggly child.

3. Make your own book about something you know your child loves. Maybe you cut out pictures of dogs and print a few words under each or maybe you make a short photo album of favourite family events. Children love to see themselves or their interests reflected in a story.

from ANNA

We thought a good nighttime routine would be to get the kids all ready for bed and then let them have their tablets for fifteen minutes. Big mistake. Taking their tablets away was always a fight, and they didn't settle down and go to sleep. They would be calling us, wanting this or that, and it was a very stressful. We decided to replace their tablets at bedtime with reading a story. It took some perseverance because the children were not happy with this change but after about three nights, I noticed they were settling down and going to sleep. No more running up the stairs four or five times to resettle them. It was working. My oldest, an eight-year-old, says she still would prefer to have the tablet, but I am hoping in time this will change.

Always keep it positive. You can't hook your child on books by force.

Reflect to Remember: A Time For Calm

- Disconnect from our busy world with a book
- Use a calm book and a calm voice
- Self-regulation is a child's ability to calm and control themselves and will help prepare them for future academic and social pursuits
- Use alternative reading ideas for the wiggly child

A Time to Seriously Connect With our Children

Maturation happens in the context of strong attached relationships with nurturing adults, who promote independence by inviting dependence. Children can develop independence when they have a strong sense of self.

Gabor Mate

Our everyday lives can be overwhelming. We live in a culture that is rapidly changing, sometimes chaotic and sometimes terrifying. Our children use devices that are addictive and tempting. They are often faced with subject matter that is beyond their understanding or is frightening.

It is more important than ever to be the one who guides your child through the craziness of life. Reading to children can help.

If we reflect on our day-to-day activities and time spent with our children, we realize there are not many opportunities to sit and engage for a sustained amount of time *every* day. We may craft one day, go for a walk, or watch a movie together, which are all wonderful activities to do with children. But how often do we repeat the same thing every day, 365 days a year? Reading books doesn't take any preparation other than planning a time to read together. It is an opportunity to sit close to your child, make eye contact, and be on the "same page."

Not only are you literally on the same page, but scientists have discovered our brains light up in the same areas when we are engaged with a story. This is called neural coupling and means the speaker's brain is synchronized with the listener's brain. Talk about being connected!

If you have established a daily reading habit, your child will know with certainty that there will be a time when mom or dad will turn off their phones, put away their other demands, and be available just for them for more than thirty seconds. This close connection is something our children crave and something they absolutely need.

Reading with your child is an amazing opportunity to be there when your child needs you, a time built into every day. Imagine your child coming in the door, and you know, just by looking at them, that all is not right in their world. You are checking the news on your phone but look up and ask, "What's wrong?" and they reply, "Nothing!" and stomp off to their room. You know something is amiss but you wait until later in the day when it's time to read together. It is quiet, they are close to you, and you begin to read. You are enjoying a story together, talking a little. You sense your child is relaxing, maybe leaning a little on you, and their breathing is slower. After another short story and a little talk, you put the book down, look at your child, and say, "How was your day?" It is the moment they need, the moment that they know you are there just for them and then that troublesome day is shared.

---

from **GRETEL:**

I think reading is an act of a loving person. That feeling of joy and connection when reading, sitting close, and cuddling just feels so good. Sometimes you have to try really hard to find a book that will work to engage your child.

As a teacher, one of my favourite activities with my students, one that I never missed no matter how busy or chaotic the day, was to read aloud to them. I loved to have them gathered around me and share our latest novel or storybook. The room was quiet, the children were attentive, and we would be transported to another world, another adventure, another life. This time was precious to me because I felt like my little school family was so connected. We would laugh together, cry together, and wonder at lives of other people and animals.

Choose Books with Intention

Select books that reflect the kind of life you want your child to live. It can be just a page in a favourite book that reinforces your values. Or maybe it is a legend or family story that has been passed on through generations. When you are reading or telling these stories, take a minute to pause, maybe add your thoughts, or ask your child what they think.

Mo Willems, Todd Parr, Eric Carle, or Paulette Bourgeois are just a few authors who write about age-appropriate experiences for very young children. You can even serve these books up at very opportune times. For instance, if your child is having trouble with friendships, choose books that demonstrate being a good friend. Pause between the pages and make it personal. Kids love to hear about their parent's lives so you might tell a personal anecdote from when you were a child. And think about the language of emotions you are using. Your child will then have the right words to express themselves about their own feelings.

Where appropriate, you might even add a little humour to help relieve the stress and tension. Something funny can enable you to handle a sensitive subject from a safe distance.

When your child is a little older, read stories that bring in a little more of the world. For instance, reading stories about animals, our planet, or children from other parts of the world which will broaden their understanding of people and the environment.

from **KATE:**

We always read at bedtime to our children, and books are a big part of our day, too. We have a library of children's books in the play area, and the children often choose to look at books on their own. Gemma is really into "pretend reading" her books.

Sometimes we check out the Free Little Libraries in our neighbourhood. My husband and I often choose to read one-on-one with a child as we feel it is a real connection point for us. We use books to help explore themes or teach about diversity. I really feel, as a family, that we have that love of reading.

Please keep this in mind: We can seek out books we think are important and have political or social agendas of which we want our children to be aware. If we constantly feed our children this type of book, reading time may feel a little heavy. Lighten up and understand that your child is a child, not an adult. They shouldn't carry the weight of the world, which they cognitively can't yet understand, on their little shoulders. The innocence of children is precious, and if we are lucky, we can visit that state of being with them on a regular basis.

I loved books about dogs. I read my students books like *Old Yeller, Shilo, Where the Red Fern Grows, Winn Dixie,* and *Stone Fox.* The students loved them too, but one year, after reading about three of these books, we were discussing what the next novel could be. Several of the children begged me, "Please, please, no more dead dogs!"

I also recall a particular student, Jacob. He was a wonderful eight-year-old who was compassionate and caring about his friends and the world. His parents were involved with local environmental initiatives and shared these with Jacob. Soon, they realized Jacob was becoming so concerned with climate change he was starting to lose sleep and become fretful. It was all he wanted to read about. They felt they needed to step back and moderate how much information Jacob was hearing about climate change. His parents chose books that were lighter. They introduced some of their childhood favourites like the *Hardy Boys*, and Jacob read the whole series. They pre-read any books about the environment and made sure they were age-appropriate and didn't contain graphic details or pictures.

It's Never Too Early

Connecting with our children doesn't have to be postponed until they are old enough to read. It can start in infancy. Connecting with our infants is so important that many NICUs encourage parents to read aloud to their newborn. Some hospitals even have special programs to prepare parents by offering tips and ideas for reading aloud. The benefits include increased bonding and less stress for the infant and the parents. Imagine your little baby being bathed in the reassuring sounds of your voice, a voice he recognizes and loves. Start with just a few seconds and increase to longer sessions, then just watch how your baby responds. You will begin to notice tiny changes in your baby, which sets you up to know your little one in such an intimate manner.

While the content of a book may not have much meaning for an infant, it won't be long before your little one can understand very simple stories and hopefully you will enjoy it too. Laughing, crying, or wondering together feels so good, and the effects of this bonding will continue far beyond your reading sessions.

In short:

> **If you want a stronger bond with your child, read together.**
>
> **If you want your child to learn about important life issues, read together.**
>
> **If you want your child to talk with you, read together.**
>
> **If you want your child to self-regulate, read together.**

from **Katie:**

In the soft light of the NICU, I sat close to the incubator which held my tiny, newborn son. He was just a wee boy but thriving and adding precious ounces every day. The anxiety and terror I had felt as they air-lifted my son to the city was gone. It was slowly replaced with a feeling that he was going to be ok, and now I could get on to the business of being a good mom. I thought, "He needs me and I am here for him."

I reached in to caress his soft downy cheek and murmured words of love, "Hello Kayden, it's your mom., I'm here. I love you and you are growing and getting to be such a big strong boy. Soon I will hold you and you will be the most loved boy ever." I reached into my bag and pulled out a big book of nursery rhymes and read to my newborn, just so he would hear my voice and know he was not alone.

Reflect to Remember:
A Time to Seriously Connect with our Children

- Reading daily is a unique and powerful activity that enables frequent connection with your child
- Our brains can synchronize when sharing books
- Have conversations during and after reading
- Choose books thoughtfully and keep children's preferences paramount
- Be careful about heavy subjects

A Time for Preparation for Academic Success

Reading aloud with children is known to be the single most important activity for building the knowledge and skills they will eventually require for learning to read.

Marilyn Jager Adams

Your economic or social status is *not* the most important predictor of academic success. It is how much time children spend reading books. Reading books for pleasure not only increases their vocabulary but also improves their concentration and ability to focus.

It doesn't stop there. Children who have been read to are more confident, have a broader general knowledge, and are better problem solvers. Their memories are stronger—think about having to recall, as you read to them, attributes of characters and details about the setting and plot.

Even children's critical and analytical thinking skills are improved. Questions from parents like "What do you think is going to happen?" or "What would you do in this situation?" or "Why did you like this book?" stimulate and validate their thinking. By doing something with joy, something that brings pleasure, you will also be preparing your child for increased literacy skills and academic success. You will wonder at the magic of this, when all you were doing was having a good time.

Building Vocabulary

Talking and reading to your child are two of the best ways to prepare your child for academic success. A child's vocabulary is built by day-to-day conversations (so talk lots with your kids) and enriched by the books that you share. Storybooks are steeped with descriptive language and unusual words that are not encountered in everyday conversation. Words such as *bulldozer, enchanting, scrumpdillitious,* or *double-decker bus* are words children will discover in their storybooks. Repeated readings will ensure that your child not only learns a new word but can actually use it. Be amazed when they use these words in everyday language like little brainiacs.

The language of emotions is also present in their storybooks, which are so important as they give children words to discuss their own feelings and more accurately, express themselves.

Does a child's vocabulary really increase that much if they listen to stories? A study conducted at Ohio State University concluded by the time a child enters Kindergarten there can be as much as a million-word gap between children who have been read to and those who haven't. Based on one book per session:

- Never Been Read To: 4,662 words
- 1-2 times per week: 63,570 words
- 3-5 times per week: 169,520 words
- Daily: 296,660 words

If you read five books per session (remember they are little books that average about 500 to 1000 words), your child would have been exposed to 1,483,300 words.

Imagine your child beginning to learn to read. They must make sense of the words they see in print using the words they understand. If they are trying to decode *bulldozer* (a pretty long word for a six-year-old), they will be much more successful if that word is part of their language.

Even more important than learning all those words is the back and forth conversations that you will have with your child. The Canadian Paediatric Society asserts that these interactions "have been more highly correlated than word quantity with a wide range of later language and cognitive skills."

Does Method Matter?

Every once in a while, headlines will appear stating children are falling behind on reading scores. This stirs up an old controversy about the best way to teach children how to read, and teachers, parents, and publishers will all push what they consider the best method. While quality instruction will benefit all students, what really matters the most is what has occurred for each child between the ages 0 to5.

An article in *Time* magazine ("What Babies and Toddlers Need to Become Good Readers") has taken a broader view and explains why ages 0 to 5 are so important for a baby's development. The article quotes paediatric surgeon Dana Suskind who says,

> What we now know of the brain demands urgency…There is neuroscientific heft about what children need, when they need it, and the essential role of parents and caregivers as children's first, best teachers.

The key word here is *urgency*. We can't wait and hope schools will magically use heavy doses of phonics or levelled readers or any other method and make our children highly literate. Early literacy, lots of talking and reading while joyously interacting with caregivers, is the best way to begin a child's literacy journey.

The other aspect that is often overlooked in this debate is joy and sustainability. If a child can read but chooses not to because they find no pleasure or excitement in the process, we really are no further ahead.

Developing Focus

When children embark on their education journey their ability to concentrate and focus will impact their growth. Children who know the joy and power of a book will also know how to sit and listen, to be attentive, and to ask questions.

Imagine those first days in kindergarten. Children are now part of a larger group and expectations for listening and paying attention are so different than in their home. It's hard not to have their needs met right away; it's hard to take turns. The teacher will help to guide the children through these changes; however, the ones who have an easier time making these adjustments are the children who have enjoyed many hours listening to stories on the laps of their parents. They have learned to stay put for the duration of a book, concentrate on one topic, and what's more, they enjoy the process.

For children who have not been read to regularly it must seem rather painful to have to sit quietly and not be engaged for ten or fifteen minutes. The teacher will observe children talking, fidgeting, or acting out in other ways. If the teacher continues to discuss the story or asks the children to draw a picture of the story, those who have been disengaged will continue to be lost. Now continue to imagine situations like this throughout the school day. A separation occurs between those children who have been read to and those who haven't.

Catching Up

Davy was a little Grade One student who stands out as an example. He was fun and enjoyed playing with the other children, and the other children enjoyed his positive energy. Watching him on the playground told me he really loved being with other kids.

In the classroom, it was a different story. He could not sit still for a story and seemed uninterested in other activities except centre time, which is a time children can freely choose a play activity. Davy usually chose active pursuits like blocks, legos, or the kitchen centre. Davy was the oldest of two boys and had two parents at home.

His mother told me that she thought reading to her child was something that was best left to teachers, so she didn't have a regular story time with either child. They did not own children's books and they did not go to a library. The family lived in a rural area far from the school, so other children, even cousin visits, were rare. Davy had not gone to preschool as the fees were not affordable. His mother said that Davy and his brother played together and she had taught them how to take turns, to share, and she did not approve of fighting. She was proud that Davy was polite and liked by the other children.

When I talked with Davy about what he liked to do at home, he said he played with his brother and watched TV. In fact, he watched a lot of TV—before school and after school. I continued to encourage Davy to engage with books. He liked the idea that he could take a book home from the library, but I'm not sure if his parents read the story to him. By December, I could see that he was slipping behind. He did not know all the names and sounds for letters, and he didn't seem to like reading time or writing time.

In January, I referred Davy for some assessments and support, and he started seeing a Learning Assistance teacher twice a week. In the class, he was polite and compliant. At book time he would get out his book, open it, and be quiet. His eyes were not on the pictures or text, and he rarely turned a page. When he got bored, he would become restless and try to engage other children in a game. The other children would sometimes get annoyed with him as they were engaged with a story and wanted to do their "work."

Learning Assistance twice a week helped a little but it soon became apparent that Davy did not like to go. By the end of the year, he knew the names of the letters but not all the sounds. He had a few favourite books but his reading level was very low. I watched Davy's progress through the primary years. He continued with Learning Assistance and remained far behind most of his peers. The bubbly little boy from Grade One also seemed less happy, and I think for Davy, school was just a chore.

Acquiring Reading Skills

When you read aloud to your child, you are *naturally* imparting information about how a book works, and that it conveys a message. Kindergarten teachers always check to see if children have this knowledge, called "Concepts of Print." If you have read to your child frequently, they will most likely have absorbed these skills. For instance, knowing where the story begins is something that is learned. Your child will have watched you read the cover page, look at the first page or two that again shows the author and the title, perhaps look at a dedication page if there is one, and then, when you turn the next page, *that* is where the story begins. If you have read hundreds of books to your child, and your child looks at books on their own, they will know this.

I am not suggesting that you approach this with a teaching attitude as it would certainly kill the pleasure of a book for most young children. Just do what you normally do, and you will have taught these important skills. Appendix II lists other skills that you will have *naturally* imparted to your child if reading aloud is part of your regular daily routine.

A Natural Progression

My daughter, Emily, was not an early reader. She was not interested in learning about letters or printing words. When she was four, she learned how to print her name but indicated no other desire to play with letters. We continued to read to her and hoped that this would change. She loved kindergarten with her young and energetic teacher, Mrs. Husband. After ten months, she knew most, but not all, the names and sounds for the letters and showed no real desire to learn them. In Grade One, she was assigned to a class with an amazing teacher, and we were hopeful. Unfortunately, her teacher was on the bargaining team for a new teacher contract and was away frequently throughout the year—sometimes for weeks at a time. The substitute teachers did the best they could, but it was not the continuity that Emily needed.

In Grade Two, she improved slowly, and we continued to read aloud every day. In Grade Three, she was placed with Mr. Johnson, whom she loved. He was an exceptional teacher and nurtured Emily to become a reader and especially a writer. By the end of Grade Three, Emily was at grade level in reading and writing and math. By Grade Eight she was on the Honor Roll.

I credit much of her learning to her amazing teachers but I also credit my husband and myself for providing her with a solid foundation in literacy, for without that, I am sure Emily would have struggled all the way through school. Emily has grown up to be a caring and dedicated teacher who helps to install the love of reading to her students.

Imagine your child eagerly anticipating story time with you, absorbing book after book, day after day, year after year. Imagine how good you will feel knowing you are giving your child so much pleasure packed with so much learning. It's like a giant present for both of you.

Reading Tip: Using Your Finger

Here's a little tip that may help you draw your child's attention to what is on the page. When you read, use your finger to slide along under the print. When you note something on the page, indicate it with your finger. It's that simple. It is important because your finger will help your child focus and concentrate. Watching your finger slide left to right will also help your child to understand that print is read in that direction.

Reflect to Remember:
A Time for Preparation for Academic Success

- Reading together helps to self-regulate children so they can sit and listen
- Increases vocabulary, comprehension, general knowledge, and memory
- Supports early literacy learning and paves the way for academic success

---

A Time for Adults Too

...a children's story which is enjoyed only by children is a bad children's story.

C.S. Lewis

For the parent who reads aloud to their children there is much to be gained. Every day you know there will be a period of calm where you can transport you and your child to an alternate world of simple characters and events. You remove yourself, for a little while, from the chaos of daily living. You will find reading to your child is a joy for you and not a chore. Your blood pressure and heart rate will go down. Amazingly, reading has been shown to reduce stress levels by 68%. That's a lot! A little gift you can give yourself every day.

The Canadian Paediatric Society states that reading aloud with your children "improved parenting style, reduced maternal depression and stress levels, enhanced parental sense of competence and self-esteem and improved parental responsiveness." And you thought you were just reading simple stories!

from KIENNA

We had a real scare when Wrenlee was a baby. She was having seizures and we were in Emergency. Wrenlee was extremely distraught and inconsolable. I was desperate to try and keep her calm and had tried just about everything. Then I remembered how much she loved this little book called *It's a Wonderful World*. I had read or sung this storybook many times. I began to sing the song from the book and amazingly Wrenlee just stopped crying and was calm. The nurses and the doctor were staring at me, and I felt so good to know I could calm my child.

The joy of children's storybooks can be enjoyed by adults who read to their children. You will realize this wonderful genre enables you to revisit childhood and a world of make-believe and wonder. Through your child you will read books you might normally never pick up but are of high interest to your child. Maybe they spark a sense of fun and frivolity or a curiosity that is new to you. Being part of a child's world is a privilege and for many, an antidote to the daily stresses of an adult's world.

Reading aloud to your child may also kindle (or rekindle) a desire to increase your own personal reading. If you are a reader, this activity has been shown to decrease mental decline, improve short-term memory and recall capabilities, and bring existing neural pathways in the brain to life. Your chances are increased for a longer life span and reducing late-life cognitive decline.

Another benefit is that when you read about characters in a story, your empathy and understanding is increased. If you meet real people with similar qualities, you are able to transfer what you learned in the story and develop better relationships. Furthermore, a benefit of routine reading before bed is that it signals to the body that you are ready to go to sleep and makes falling asleep easier.

If you are a reader, you will also be modelling this activity for your children. Remember that children mimic what their parents do. I can't stress this enough—what you *do* really counts.

Finally, reading aloud to your child will give you a sense of accomplishment, a feeling that you are doing something really good for your child. We all want to make children's lives more fulfilling, more fun, more meaningful. Whether you are a parent, a grandparent, a caregiver, or a friend, reading aloud is an important avenue to achieve this goal.

Reflect to Remember:
Reading is Good For Adults Too

- A time for fun, relaxation, and de-stressing
- A feeling of accomplishment as a parent
- Being a reader yourself has many benefits

DETAILS: WHO, WHERE, WHEN

*Show me a family of readers and I will show
you the people who move the world.*

Napoleon Bonaparte

Let's talk about some basic details that will help you become an amazing read-aloud parent. You will learn **who** should read to a child, **where** you can read, and **when** and how long to read.

Who Should Read to a Child?

While moms and dads are often the ones who most frequently read aloud, caregivers, teachers, grandparents and siblings can all get involved.

If all these people model reading aloud as something important and fun, imagine the huge impact on the child. Children will experience different styles and conversations, material and ideas, and it will greatly enrich their lives.

The Reading Mother
by Strickland Gillilan

I had a mother who read to me
Sagas of pirates who scoured the sea,
Cutlasses clenched in their yellow teeth,
"Blackbirds" stowed in the hold beneath.

I had a Mother who read me lays
Of ancient and gallant and golden days;
Stories of Marmion and Ivanhoe,
Which every boy has a right to know.

I had a Mother who read me tales
Of Gelert the hound of the hills of Wales,
True to his trust till his tragic death,
Faithfulness blent with his final breath.

I had a Mother who read me the things
That wholesome life to the boy heart brings—
Stories that stir with an upward touch,
Oh, that each mother of boys were such!

You may have tangible wealth untold;
Caskets of jewels and coffers of gold.
Richer than I you can never be—
I had a Mother who read to me.

Parents

If there are two parents in the home, it is great if reading aloud is shared, as both parents will offer different styles and approaches. Aside from the positive role modelling (which should not be underestimated), one parent may discuss topics in a more practical way that extends children's understanding. Each parent might choose different reading material so children can encounter a whole new category of vocabulary. One parent may make sounds for just about anything and a quiet reading session will not usually happen. If there is a bulldozer in the story, be prepared for bulldozer sounds; a dog, you'll hear yapping; a mean monster, you'll hear scary growls. Each parent's unique brand of humour often leads to lots of giggles and boisterous reading sessions. Parents who are able to connect emotionally with the contents of a book and share this with their children can have a profound effect on their children's emotional lives.

from CHRIS:

When Audrey is busy, say making dinner, then I have both children. We sit on the couch, one on either side. Ava is seven months and Cullen is three, and Cullen has learned he has to turn the pages. He really likes books, and I can see how the stories we read often transfer to his playtime. Books are a way I can be involved with my kids.

Grandparents

Grandparents have a unique opportunity to help shape the lives of their grandchildren through reading aloud. Grandparents who live miles or continents away can connect through a Zoom-type platform and read to their grandchildren. And even if you live in the same city, use technology to read at night to your grandchildren and maybe give mom or dad a break. Grandparents are often in a position where their daily demands are less, and they can really spend some quality time with their grandchildren.

I have several friends who read aloud to their grandchildren on a regular basis. I can tell they are so proud to report the latest developments of how reading aloud has enhanced their interactions and how incredibly "smart," "cute," "adorable," or "calm" their grandchildren are with books. Regina's three-year-old granddaughter Arly is fond of reenacting a book with her dolls and will switch voices for different characters and even as the narrator. Regina says she takes on a flatter tone as she says, "the princess replied" or "the princess wondered."

Arly's brother Finn is really into spiders and has a prodigious memory for all facts about spiders. He tells you, "The wolf spider is the scariest looking spider but if you turn ahead three pages you will see the meanest spider." Then he will go on to detail facts about each spider.

My friend Brenda is astounded by her grandson Eli who loves to look at adult books about the moon. His ability to self-regulate with books is amazing. These grandparents all credit reading aloud as a powerful way to establish truly positive and meaningful relationships.

from **REGINA:**

It is not easy keeping up with my grandchildren's energy levels, and I am so grateful that book sharing, a less physical activity, is something we all love.

Siblings

Older siblings have an opportunity to be a role model and practice their reading skills by reading simple books to a brother or sister. Younger siblings often look up to a cool, older brother or sister, and the positive connections can last a lifetime. After all, a sibling relationship is often the longest relationship we will ever have.

Others

Ask anyone who cares for your child to make sure reading books is a priority. Have a book bag filled with your child's favourites, something familiar and cherished, which can help ease anxiety and loneliness while your child is separated from you.

The more people who read aloud to your child, the better. Children will experience different styles and conversations, material and ideas, all of which will enrich their lives.

Your child will enjoy the storytelling talents of a librarian or teacher, so make sure to ask about the novels or storybooks they hear.

from CATHERINE:

In my family we all read. My kids really like reading, and I think we have books in just about every room. I usually read aloud as part of our bedtime routine. My husband never really liked reading aloud, but now I notice, especially with the youngest, he will say, "Garret, go get a book," and they will read together and he loves it.

Reflect to Remember: Who Should Read to a Child?

- Parents top the list
- Grandparents have a unique position to make reading aloud extra special
- Siblings can establish positive bonds by reading together
- Don't forget to ask caregivers to read aloud
- Listen to a talented storyteller, such as a librarian

Where Is the Best Place To Read to a Child?

Books are a uniquely portable magic.
Stephen King

Reading a book at bedtime, when children are tucked warmly under the covers, is a favourite time and place for many families, but it needn't be the only place.

In Your Home

While your child is having a bath
At the dinner table
On a swing or in a tent in the backyard
A cozy tent of blankets in the living room
In a big comfy chair
Under a table

Away From Home

An audio story for car rides, long or short.
Doctor's office, restaurant, hospital, church...
Under a tree at a park.
At the beach.
Bus, train, ferry...
At the cottage

If a book is unavailable, consider the fact that you have a wealth of stories inside of you—stories about your youth, your children's births, or what they were like when they were little. Funny stories or romantic stories about how you met their dad...Children love to hear these stories, and it is part of the special glue that unites your family. The chapter on Oral Storytelling will provide further information on its importance and how-to suggestions.

from **BRANT:**

I learned about reading to your children in a parenting book. My daughter Harper loves stories. I like to read to her before bed because it calms her down and she doesn't fight bedtime.

Reflect to Remember:
Where is the Best Place to Read to a Child?

- Peacefully tucked into bed and looking forward to hearing a story
- Consider other places in your home
- Don't forget the book bag when you are away from home—many opportunities will occur that are perfect for a mini-read
- Tell your own stories

When and for How Long?

I will defend the importance of bedtime
stories to my last gasp.

J.K.Rowling

When to start? What time of day? For how many minutes should I read? At what age should I stop reading aloud? The answers to each of these questions will be particular to your family and the schedules of your children. This section will give you some suggestions and ideas to make reading aloud and sharing books an everyday occurrence.

My personal journey for reading aloud to Emily began with a few bumps. I was just a new mom. I was going to read to my daughter starting the day I came home from the hospital. The drive, normally ninety minutes, was an arduous and slow two-and-a-half hours on a snowy November night. Emily wailed almost the whole way home, and I was exhausted. My nipples were sore, my body ached, I felt like a fog had enveloped me. Sleep was what I craved. No read-aloud that night. Or for the next few weeks. When my husband asked what I did during the day, I would think about it and honestly reply, "I fed the baby." That was it. I fed the baby.

Gradually I slept a little, felt more connected to the world, and then remembered my plan to read aloud to Emily. What do I read? Someone had suggested that it didn't really matter what you read. I grabbed a mystery novel that I had started before Emily was born. I snuggled into the big, comfy rocker, nursed her, and then proceeded to read aloud. In a sing-song voice, I read about detectives discovering bodies, descriptions of unsavoury characters, and pathologists talking about the contents of a stomach. Here was my perfect, innocent newborn, wide awake, seemingly listening and I was reading a really gruesome novel. I thought, "This isn't going to work." Not only was I not getting the thread of the text but I was feeling like a bad mom introducing ideas to her that were so frightening. Any text may work for some parents, but it wasn't going to work for me.

I was still committed to reading to my daughter but the next time I grabbed *Goodnight Moon*. She still didn't understand what was going on, but she was snuggled next to me, all warm and cozy, hearing her mom's voice in a light and rhythmical tone. Content. Quiet. Perfect.

When to Start

It is ideal to begin reading aloud when your child is an infant. A baby experiences their most rapid brain growth from birth to about age three, so parents will want to make the most of this time. An infant will not comprehend a story, but they will connect and be soothed with the sound of your voice and the rhythm of language. They will learn to look, point, and touch. Snuggling with your baby and the sound of your voice signals safety, love, and connection, which is the perfect environment for your little one to learn.

from PAULINE:

I read *Knuffle Bunny* to Wyatt when he was about eighteen months. I could see that he was thinking very hard, and then all of a sudden he grabbed my arm and pulled me into his room and pointed to his Bunny in the crib. He wanted to have it while we read the story! He was making connections even though he didn't have the language. I need to be confident that he is doing that all the time even though it may not be apparent.

Once again, let me remind you, if you don't begin reading to your child as infant, all is not lost. It is never too early or too late to begin reading aloud. Maybe your child is two, five, or even nine, and you feel you should start reading aloud. What often happens is you, the parent, get all charged up and approach your child saying, "We are going to read together every day for twenty minutes, starting right now." I'll bet you'll get a reaction that is less than favourable. So, spend a little time thinking about the best way to implement a daily read-aloud.

The process of forming a habit has been meticulously documented in a book called *Atomic Habits* by James

Clear. The following ideas have been heavily borrowed from this text.

Be clear about your intention—"I will read aloud at (time) in (location)." Remember that you are not the only one trying to form this habit so as much as possible, include your child in this decision. They should know why you think it is important and can contribute to the when and where of the intention.

Next, try to pair reading aloud with an old habit you have already established. For instance,

- On our ride to the school, we will listen to an audio story
- When you take a bath, I will read to you
- When we finish dinner, we will stay at the table and read together
- When you get tucked into bed, I will read you a bedtime story

Don't be concerned with the length of time spent reading, especially at the beginning. If you only pick up a book and talk about it, consider that a win. If you only have time for one page, consider that a win. Some days you and your child will be pressed for time and other days you may lose track of time and read for thirty minutes.

Another way to increase your success is to make sure you have books...lots of them. And not just books— newspapers, magazines, pamphlets, flyers...If you find a minute, pick up a book or magazine and start reading. The section "What to Read: All About Books" will give you some ideas where to find books. Outings with your child to garage sales, used bookstores, or markets are a fun and inclusive way to build the reading habit and your own home library.

All that reading material needs a place to go, so have a dedicated shelf for books in your child's room but also strategically place them all over the house:

- Coffee-table books in the living room
- Magazines in the bedrooms
- Joke books in the bathroom
- Poetry books on the front porch
- Cookbooks and magazines in the kitchen
- Storybooks everywhere

Saturate your environment with books, and you will be more likely to become a family that reads together.

Some children may think reading is boring or nerdy. They need to be aware that the culture of reading is global. Show them who reads. Look at online book clubs for kids or talk about influential adults who read—Reese Witherspoon, Michelle Obama, LeBron James, Malala Yousafzai, Emma Watson, and Bill Gates, just to name a few.

When you first start to cultivate this habit, you may need to give you and your child visible, positive reinforcement. Tracking your read-aloud sessions—x's on the calendar or marbles in a jar are immediately satisfying. You may want to follow up with a bigger incentive once you have cumulated a pre-determined amount of marbles or x's. A trip to a local bookstore to buy a book, an outing to someplace you read about, or making the same type of cookies that Mama Berenstein Bear made are fun and celebratory ways to keep encouraging this new habit.

A final piece of advice from *Atomic Habits* author James Clear is never miss twice. If you miss a day, get right back on track the next day.

Time of Day

Time of day is particular to each family. Some families have a designated book time, like twenty minutes after supper. No devices, just books. Some families like bedtime. Some families have no particular schedule but still make a point to include it daily. Find what works for your family. The demands on a young person's time often leave precious little time for reading.

Let your child see how you include reading throughout the day. They probably see you reading at home but also let them see you pulling out a book while waiting for appointments, at the hair salon, waiting for the bus, or while in the car. These are good examples of mini-reading moments. They add up. And sometimes there will be that book that you just can't put down and you read for two hours. (How is that possible? How did you find the time? What did you not do?—all good questions to reflect on.) If you are serious about reading, you make time.

If you are really having difficulty finding a time to read, look carefully at how your children spend their days. Sometimes we are over-scheduling our children, and they do not have enough down time at home. Is there something you could change? Many parents feel overscheduled at well. While changing this might not be possible, consider other people your child sees during the day. Ask your child's caregivers to include reading to your child. Enlist a grandparent or other relative to help make reading aloud a daily treat.

from **KRISTA:**

I find that reading at bedtime is often the only time I have during a day. When we had one or two children, we would read at different times but with four children, I need Joe's help. We have included story time in their nighttime routine. The kids are in their pjs, the business of the day is done, and the children look forward to this last event with both of us.

How Many Minutes?

A successful reading time may be just thirty seconds if you have a wiggly child, or it may be fifteen to twenty minutes for older children. What works one day may need to be modified the next. Be flexible. You need to take your cues from your child and most importantly, this needs to be pleasurable. If it feels onerous, no one is going to feel good or want to do it again. Bedtime reading is usually a set amount of time or a set number of books.

Make sure your child knows the rule or they may keep asking for another book!

Summer Reading

One final consideration. For many children, the close of school for the summer is an end to all literacy, and it can create a real void and academic loss. By continuing to read aloud to your child (and encouraging the habit of reading for themselves) you can help to curtail any literacy losses they might have over the summer.

Reflect to Remember: When and For How Long?

- Infancy is the best time to begin reading aloud
- Choose the best time of day, according to your family's schedules and needs
- Time spent reading aloud can vary from day to day and from child to child
- Summer is an important time to ramp up your read-aloud

When To Stop Reading Aloud

The joy of reading with our children doesn't stop when they, and we, get older, it simply changes.

Paul Kroop

When do I stop? I want to say "never" but perhaps a more practical answer is when your child indicates they no longer want to read together. And even then, check in periodically, and ask, "Do you want to read together tonight?"

Many parents mistakenly believe when their child can read their own text, the read-aloud is no longer necessary. A survey conducted by *Scholastic* in 2016 confirmed that parents reading to children dropped significantly around age six; however, 85% of the children, aged six to fourteen who are still being read aloud to, say they loved it. The kids say "It's a special time with my parent," "Reading together is fun," and "It's relaxing to be read to before I go to sleep."

Recall all those reasons to read aloud listed in the opening sections of this book: preparing for academic success, connection, calm, fun, and personal benefits for adults. These benefits do not magically disappear just because your child has learned to decode the squiggles on the page. In fact, reading aloud to your child is as important as ever. A few adaptations for older children is all you need.

Perhaps the most compelling reason to continue to read with your child is to keep your proximity close, to know what is going on in their world, and to continue to guide them in a loving and non-authoritarian manner.

For older children, thinking of reading as a fun activity will not be the same as when they were four or six. As children get older and more independent, there are other things vying for their attention—friends, sports activities, technology, special clubs, school, and hobbies to name a few. They have a limited amount of leisure time, so it is important to keep reading a priority because you know how great an impact it can have on their lives. Share some of these reasons from time to time with your child.

Perhaps the most important thing you can do is to continue to model reading. I know I've mentioned this a few times, but if your child sees you reading for pleasure, talking about the books you've read, or how excited you get when you come home from the library or bookstore, it will have an impact on them. They need to see that reading matters, you gain pleasure from it, and you are constantly learning. In other words, you don't just say that reading is important—you need to be a living, breathing, shining example of a reading enthusiast. Think of all the compelling reasons that have been previously listed as benefits of reading aloud. Now that your child is older, those reasons still exist and in fact take on a different importance. Let's revisit them.

A Time for Fun

Interestingly, the time that most parents stop reading to their children is around eight years old, and that is the same age that a drop in reading for pleasure occurs. Have books been a shared pleasure? A source of fun? A time to laugh together? Your older child may not laugh uncontrollably at nonsense words anymore, but I'm sure they still have a sense of humour and a sense of fun. Look for new ways to tap into this—new books, new genres, new conversations.

A Time for Calm

Many school-age children spend their days engaged in school, activities, practices, and one event after another. Then they fall into bed exhausted. That's just not a healthy or advantageous life for a child (or anyone, for that matter). We will not meet their basic needs by over-scheduling and exhausting our kids. They need a consistent quiet time in their busy days to connect with a loved one, and regular reading together will help your child feel some control and help create a sense of calm. An interesting or thoughtful book will help your child re-engage with favourite characters and themes, and allow them to let go of the daily grind of their day. Sitting beside a loving parent and sharing a book will bring about quiet and calm, and it may lead into some much-needed time to connect.

A Time For Seriously Connecting With Our Children

Once we have established that calm time with our children, we are better able to discuss difficult issues and continue to create a strong family bond. Books that you would not have read when they were younger because of mature content can now be explored and discussed. Books with problems like family illness, drug use, romantic relationships, facing climate change, or peer pressure are all on the table for discussion. And sometimes it's easier or safer to discuss a character's problems than your own. Having a loving adult to discuss these issues is a much-needed antidote in a culture where peers and social media can be all too prevalent in forming a young person's ideas. Some current adolescent and teen fiction can be an eye-opener that may enable you to understand your child's world a little better. Touchy topics are often easier to discuss through the characters or theme of a book.

A Time for Preparation for Academic Success

Listening to fiction or non-fiction can help improve the understanding of the text. Thinking deeply and interacting with a text during school hours is constrained by time, and your child may not have the opportunity to ask questions or be part of a conversation. When you read one-on-one, they have that time. They will benefit by exploring new vocabulary, learning about the world, and increasing their attention span. By reading texts they choose, you can stimulate their curiosity and prepare them for lifelong learning.

A Time for Adults to Benefit

As our children get older, they spend more time with friends and that influence is not always good. If we continue to read or share books with our children, we also continue to have an avenue for communication. As adults we benefit by having an opportunity that is pleasurable for you and your child as well as a time for some heartfelt talks. We want to hang on to our kids. Maintaining a book time with your older child will also be less time for your child (or you!) to be on your phones.

from KATIE

I started reading to Kayden when he was in my womb. When he was young, we would get milk and cookies, turn the lights down low, and read. Kayden has his own personal library. He is now in middle school, and we still read together. Sometimes he likes to read to me.

Reflect to Remember: When to Stop Reading Aloud?

- Don't assume older children outgrown or do not enjoy a daily read aloud time
- Continue to read aloud to keep your proximity close
- Modelling reading has a huge impact
- Older children continue to benefit in many ways from a read aloud time with a loving adult

WHAT TO READ: ALL ABOUT BOOKS!

The only thing that you absolutely have to know is the location of the library.
Albert Einstein

Here you will learn where to get books, where to get book recommendations, and what kind of books to read at specific ages.

Where To Get Books

Libraries are perhaps one of our greatest assets. The idea that you can get a book for free, return it, and get more is life-changing for many people. Libraries are important community centres and free public spaces that welcome all and offer a cornucopia of resources and services. As if this couldn't get any better, they are usually staffed by people who are knowledgeable and love to help. Unfortunately, not all libraries are the same and not all are located in areas of greatest need. Low-income areas are often the most poorly served. Limited hours, poor quality resources, non-professional staff, and few books are just some of the problems. We must continue to advocate for this important public service and understand that libraries are needed now more than ever to serve a diverse population.

---

from **BRENDA:**

Every Friday, I would look after my grandson and take him for a walk in his stroller. We always took the same route, and one day when we were passing the library, he pointed to the building and was trying to say something. I said yes, that was the library, and he kept pointing and babbling. Later, when I asked my daughter if he went to the library, she explained that her husband had been taking Eli to the library once a week, and they both loved it. Eli was not even a one-year-old, and he knew about the wonders of a library!

Your child's school library may offer lending privileges to parents, books fairs, and some free books. School librarians can also offer suggestions on great books for kids.

Access to books is essential. If you can afford to buy books there are many stores that sell children's books— book stores, grocery stores, pharmacies, department stores. Amazon, Indigo, Book Outlet, Bookshop, and

Costco are a few online book sellers. Many communities have second-hand bookstores, and don't forget to look at yard sales, Craigslist, and local parent swaps on Facebook.

A child's personal library, complete with their favourite books, is a treasure. Investing in a home library for your child has a huge influence on their future levels of education. In fact, it is more influential than having rich or well-educated parents. The more books you have in your home, the greater the benefit. Think of creating a home library as investing in your child's future.

Consider Oprah Winfrey. She was raised in poverty and had a very difficult early life. Books from a local library constantly filled her home. She recalls,

> Books were my pass to personal freedom. I learned to read at age three, and soon discovered there was a whole world to conquer that went beyond our farm in Mississippi. Books showed me there were possibilities in life, that there were actually people like me living in a world I could not only aspire to but attain. Reading gave me hope. For me, it was the open door.

Another place to look for books might just be a few doors away. Free Little Libraries is a non-profit organization that promotes neighbourhood book exchanges. These are usually small wooden boxes on the edge of someone's property. Anyone may take a book or leave a book to share.

One of the greatest assets of a Free Little Library is how connected you become to other people in your community. The first day we put up our little library, I was surprised by how many people stopped by to have a look. The next day I noticed people taking books and others bringing books. When I am in the garden and someone comes to our book box, we strike up a conversation and learn a little more about each other and our neighbours. We live on a road that children pass by on their way to and from school, so I have been sure to put out children's books and maybe hook a young person on a great book.

What about online stories? Screen time is not recommended for children under two years old and if you choose to share these stories with an older child, it is best done together. Consider these stories as an occasional alternative and remember, the real power of reading with your children will always be your presence and connection. (Studies of online vs parent-read stories show little benefit from an online story. More on this subject in the technology section.)

Dolly Parton's Imagination Library is a free service offered to children from birth to five. Every month a free children's book arrives in the mail. Dolly started this service in her home state of Tennessee in recognition of the importance of reading and later life success. Imagination Libraries are in all parts of the world, sponsored by local organizations. Check to see if this service is offered in your area. There are other similar organizations offering free books, but it may take a little digging to find out what is available. Teachers, your family doctor, or public health nurse may have more information on this topic.

Many communities have a Literacy Centre that help adults and children with low literacy. Even countries like Canada and United States, where most adults are considered literate, an alarming percentage, over 40%, are considered "low literate." This means they may have trouble filling out forms or comprehending the written or spoken word. Often it will take them much longer to read a passage or they will need to reread. Literacy centres often have many free books or can help you with some ideas for acquiring books.

from **MARY M:**

In our family, my husband managed online book buying. Our kids knew books were something we would always purchase for them; they only had to ask. Many books are available new or used. We felt providing books to our kids in a timely manner was a way to keep them reading.

The Value of a Book Recommendation

*You are not finished a book until you pass it
to another reader.*

Donalyn Miller

Personal Recommendations

Don't be afraid to suggest a book you think your child may enjoy. A few words about the book, highlighting some parts you think will hook your child, is one of the best ways to encourage reading. Think of the success Oprah had with her book club. She would give an enthusiastic description of a book and presto!—thousands of people ran out and bought that book. As a reader myself, I have friends and family that I share books with, and we talk about our latest reads. Your child needs some community as well. Maybe it's their family or maybe they have a friend who enjoys the same kind of books and they can share.

Teachers and Librarians

Teachers and librarians need to "sell" books to kids. They know that a few enticing words about the book and showing a page or two (this is called a *book talk*) is one of the best ways to get kids to choose a book. Check out their school library. Talk with the librarian and your child's teacher. They are great resources for what is popular and "in."

Often children (and adults) like to browse a library or bookstore and can be hooked on a title or interesting cover. Make sure if you do pick up that interesting cover or title, you give the book a good preview, especially if you are putting out hard-earned cash!

from EMILY

The novels I read aloud are often the books that my students will re-read. They also like to see if there are other books by the same author. A favourite is *The Christmas Pig* by JK Rowling. One year I didn't finish it in time for winter vacation and many of my students told me they had received it as a Christmas gift. That tells me they had talked to their parents about the book and loved it so much they wanted their own copy. It also turned some of my students on to the *Harry Potter* series by the same author.

Book Communities

Some kids like online book communities like Goodreads or various book clubs on social media. Radio programs like CBC's *The Next Chapter* with Shelia Rogers or a multitude of book podcasts are other ways to learn about new books.

What Shall I Read?

*Fill your house with stacks of books, in all
the crannies and all the nooks.*

Dr. Seuss

There are millions of children's books. Where do you start? What books are most appealing to your child at different ages? Appendix I will list some specific titles for certain ages but below is a general guideline.

Ages 0-2

When your child is an infant, you will be doing all the choosing. Soft fabric books are wonderful as baby can spit, suck, or crinkle them, and you can just throw the book in the wash. Board books are also popular as they are more durable. The text in these books tend to be very short or not necessarily an entire story. One picture, one word. You can read just about anything when babies are very young. They may not understand what you are saying but just the sound or your voice and being close is what they need.

As babies learn to hold and manipulate objects they can also learn to handle books. Nursery rhymes are great when your child gets a little older as they will enjoy the natural rhythm of these little poems. Have little conversations about the book. Ask, "Do you see the dog?

Encourage your child to point, and if they point at something, talk about it. Your conversations may seem very one-sided but science is telling us that babies are absorbing so much at this age so go ahead, chat away.

Soon your baby will be babbling along and it will begin to feel like a conversation!

Before you know it, your child will be able to start self-selecting their favourite books. A friend told me that her ten-month-old grandson would grunt and point at the book he wanted. As we stated earlier, it is very important to honour a child's choices in books. It means you may be reading a book that you don't particularly like, or reading the same book over and over and over again, but by honouring your child's choices, you are supporting and confirming their ability to make choices that are appropriate for their age level. You will also be ensuring that reading books remains fun and therefore more likely to last a lifetime. Keep in mind the particular interests of your child and find books to match. Keep it light, keep it fun.

Age 2

Two-year-old children like stories about things that are familiar to them; such as brushing their teeth, helping mom, walking the dog, or playing with toys. Some books are interactive and have flaps to lift or textures to touch and little ones really love these books. Don't forget to ask questions and really look at the pictures.

from PAULINE:

Wyatt (aged 2) loves to read with Grandpa, and I have noticed that it is usually the same five books every time. Maybe he thinks Grandpa is the best storyteller for those books. I have to credit my husband for his patience. I know children love to listen to the same story many times. We feel more connected to our grandkids and enjoy helping out.

Age 3

At about three, your child will be interested in stories with simple plots. They have a beginning, middle, and end, and usually have a problem to solve. Vocabulary is more complex, and the feelings of the characters are good discussion points with your child. Children at this age are also keen for non-fiction books that reflect their areas of interest.

Stories about other children or animals are popular, as are naming books (books about colours, things that go, kitchen items, toys, trucks, etc.) Repetitive and rhyming texts are fun and enjoyable for children this age.

from REGINA:

Finn loves books and he will often pick his favourites and that is all he wants to read. For a while he only chose books about dinosaurs. Dinosaurs became his world and he would play games about dinosaurs, talk about dinosaurs and pretend to be a dinosaur. His level of knowledge was amazing and I actually took an online course on dinosaurs to try and keep up with him!

Ages 4-5

You will notice that your child at ages four and five is able to listen to longer and more complex stories. Some children are able to comprehend simple novels at around age five, and you might try one with your child. If they are not interested, do not force it. A short novel like *Fantastic Mr. Fox* by Roald Dahl has short chapters, lots of action, pencil drawings, and lends itself to expressive reading. But don't forget the picture book; they are really suitable for all ages, and older children love to revisit old favourites.

Ages 6-8

Children of this age can listen to longer, more complex novels yet still love picture books, so be sure to include both. When choosing books for this age, think animal, humour, and excitement. Animal adventures such as *The Mouse and the Motorcycle*, *Charlotte's Web*, or the *Mercy Watson* series are great. Humour is a must for some children this age, and there are plenty of books to tickle the funny bone. Try *Kung Pow Chicken* or *The Bad Guys*. Children find most novels by Roald Dahl exciting but also try the *Dragon Master* series.

Ages 8-10

At this age, children are becoming more independent and enjoy the company of their peers. It is a good time to offer different genres, from fantasy to heartfelt stories, and see what resonates. Animal stories such as *The Tale of Despereaux* (exciting) or *The One and Only Ivan* (heartfelt) are popular. *Diary of a Wimpy Kid* or *Gangsta Granny* are sure to be amusing. Graphic novels also seem appealing and the *Amulet* or *Hilo* series are good ones to check out.

Anything by Michael Morpurgo, Roald Dahl, or Sarah Pennypacker may also please your child. At this age, children will start to look for other books an author has written, so it is great to find an author who has written many novels.

The picture book, that wonderful mainstay of reading to young children, now takes on a different appeal. Did you know that many picture books are not written for young children? The content of these books is engaging, thought provoking, and only suitable for an older audience. Discussions generated from these texts are deep and meaningful. And, because they are short, your child may reread them to themselves later and find even more depth and wonder. One meaningful book for older children is called *Faithful Elephants, The True Story of Animals, People and War* by Yukio Tsuchiya. I would read it aloud around Remembrance Day because it captures a different aspect of the devastating effects of war. The story takes place at a zoo in Tokyo and the zookeepers are wondering what they should do about the elephants in light of the impending bombing. It evokes compassion, empathy, and deep conversations.

Picture books often come with wonderful works of art that contain a great deal of information.

A final word on picture books. They are sometimes placed in a section of the library called "Easy Fiction." Many school librarians have changed that title to "Forever Fiction" for at least two reasons:

1. Some picture books are not written for really young children. The content, vocabulary, and interest are for more mature minds.
2. Some children will not pick up an Easy Fiction book because they consider it a "baby" book and to be seen with such a book will reflect poorly on their ability.

Rethink the picture book as more of a form of writing rather than relegating it to an age group. You'll be glad you did!

Ages 10-12

As independence and interactions with their peers grow, it is a good time to continue reading with your child. The outside world is increasingly interesting. Your child will start to recognize cause and effect sequences and be able to critique stories and think logically.

Try the *Percy Jackson, Eragon,* or the *Golden Compass* series if your child enjoys fantasy or magic. For non-fiction lovers, *I am Malala* or *Hidden Figures* (young reader's edition) are favourites. *Where the Mountain Meets the Moon,* or *The Westing Game* will appeal to those who enjoy mystery and adventure. Coming of age stories such as *Touching Spirit Bear, Al Capone Does My Shirts,* or *Restart* are notable.

Fiction and Non-Fiction

Books fall into two main categories: fiction and non-fiction. Fortunately, the children's publishing industry embraces both. Fiction is an imagined account of people and events, and non-fiction is based on truth and accuracy, although it may be biased. Both have a place and a purpose in what we choose to read. One is not better than the other, just different.

Benefits of Fiction

The length of time it takes to sit with a character in a novel will allow us to deepen our understanding and compare the human experience with that of our own. Standing in another's shoes for longer than a page or two can increase our empathy and compassion for others in similar situations. The author often examines other character's perspectives to the same problem, which can be useful in fully understanding a problem and seeing the big picture. Even a short children's book like *Franklin the Turtle* will show how a problem can occur and the process and thinking around solving it.

Problem solving in fiction allows us to see how problems are created, and the process one might go through in solving problems. It is often not quick, it evolves at a pace that includes trial and error, reflection, consultation, personal angst, and a myriad of other behaviours. It is human.

Dads reading fiction to their children, especially their sons, allows for some emotional conversations that are sometimes hard for men. On the laps of their fathers, boys can learn about their emotions and their dad, their most trusted, male model, has a very important and influential role to play. Giving a voice and vocabulary for their thoughts and feelings is so important for their emotional growth.

Unlike memoirs or biographies that tell a story about a human condition, (sometimes through the benefit of hindsight or fabrication), an author of a novel needs to craft and reflect on their characters' emotions and actions. Biographies are often a fractured and selective account of the events in a person's life and sometimes without a lot of insight or emotional reflection. A work of fiction is a carefully written and thoughtful account of how a person thinks and behaves. An author is not tempted to remove the ugly, not-so-proud moments of a life.

Fiction helps to focus and retain a complex story for a longer period of time, and often involves reflection or thinking about the story line or a character's behaviour. In a world of "short and snappy," this is a much-needed gift.

Brain scans have revealed that the brain responds to a story in more areas than factual information. Researchers have found our brain can feel what a character in a book can feel. We can imagine what another person is feeling and become more empathic.

Finally, a chapter book can give us companionship, an escape, and enrich our lives.

Benefits of Non-Fiction

And now a few words on non-fiction. Children are naturally curious about the world around them. Their interests can be enhanced through the wonderful world of children's non-fiction books.

The vocabulary—oh, the vocabulary! It's amazing to hear a three-year-old rattle off, flawlessly, the various names of snakes, dinosaurs or machines. Their minds act like little sponges for all that information.

Some parents who may be reluctant to read aloud often find sharing non-fiction a great way to read with their children. Share your own interests as well as your child's.

Really savour the pictures or graphics—spend time with children discussing the details of a page and the information it conveys.

Notice that you read non-fiction differently than fiction—re-reading, pondering on one page for a long time, reading only part of the book—so this is not necessarily a beginning-to-end-in-one-session book.

Notice how a page might be laid out differently than a simple story. There might be boxes for little nuggets of information, arrows pointing to pictures, or different sizes and fonts for text. Exploring these books helps prepare your child for reading textbooks later in school.

Non-fiction will help reinforce the distinction between real and make-believe and it lays the foundation for being a critical reader and thinker. Most children's books are well-researched and curated, but be aware of older texts that have outdated information—i.e., Pluto is no longer a planet—and use this as teachable moment to talk about fact-checking information. Also be aware of texts that show obvious bias and use it as a teachable moment.

Non-fiction prompts further questions and raises awareness—ie., importance of exercise and healthy eating, recycling, conservation, and so forth.

You may start to read a book and find it doesn't appeal to you or your child. Have a little discussion about why you don't like it, and know that you are under no obligation to finish it.

Reflect To Remember: All About Books!

- From libraries to garage sales, there are many places to acquire books
- Use personal book recommendations
- It's important to choose the right type of book according to your child's age
- Two main categories of books, fiction and non-fiction, offer something for everyone

How To Read Aloud

You're never too old, too wacky, too wild,
to pick up a book and read to a child.

Dr. Seuss

Reading aloud may only require the ability to read; however, there are so many ways in which you can enrich the reading. Practice will certainly improve this skill and additionally, this section will present some practical ideas that you can try tonight. Here, I'll offer ideas on how to read with expression; paying attention to the title, first, and last lines; and how to really look at those pictures. You will also learn how to talk through a book and the importance of repetition.

How To Read With Expression

The impact of using expression cannot always be measured but I had an experience that reminded me of its power. Several years ago, I gave my niece, Brielle, a new book for her third birthday. She asked me to read it to her. I hesitated because there were several adults as well as older children in the room, and I knew the way to read that particular story was with plenty of expression. My heart was pounding, and I was suddenly self-conscious all over again. *Would I sound stupid? Look ridiculous? Would the adults think I was showing off?* I knew I could not refuse to read the book, and after a quick little pep talk to myself, I read with gusto and abandon. Loud voices, soft voices, scary voices, baby voices…it was all in this book.

Brielle never said a word throughout the whole story but just stared at me with very big, deer-in-the-headlights eyes. It unnerved me to the point where several times throughout the book I considered putting it down. *Was she scared? Was I terrifying her?* Brielle never took her eyes off me and so I continued. If she was really frightened, she would have run to her mom or dad, both of whom were in the room. I persevered through the whole book, but was relieved when I came to the end, and we went on to something else. It left me a little confused about whether my reading was a little "over the top" and maybe I should have toned it down. I really wasn't sure what had been going on for Brielle.

My answer came about a week later, when I received a short video from my niece's mom. Brielle was alone on the carpet reading the birthday book. This wee little girl with strawberry-red hair in a pretty, little, blue dress was totally engaged and so animated. She was making up the words and using all the expressions that I had used at her birthday party. As she turned each page, she would look carefully at the pictures and verbalize in different voices her memory of its meaning. She was happy! She was having a good time!

The emotional impact of hearing the book read with expression had enabled Brielle, a non-reader, to remember the context of each page enough to tell the story. It warmed my heart and reminded me never to feel awkward about reading expressively to children because it makes a difference and is, of course, s-o-o-o-o fun!

Don't you just open a book and start to read? Well, yes. And no. If you really want to engage your child, there is a little more to it—using expression is an enhancement that can make or break a good reading session.

Parents use a special type of voice (called Parent-ese) when they are speaking to their babies. It is higher pitched and natural when speaking to an infant. We use this voice because our babies engage more with us when we do. Continue to use this voice when you are reading to your baby, and you will find they really are more engaged. Don't forget to look at your baby, and use your face and body to express emotion as well—big eyes, open mouth, smile, raise those eyebrows, wave those arms…

When your child is a little older and enjoys nursery rhymes and simple stories, try adjusting your tone or volume according to the story:

Jack and Jill went up *(have your voice go up)* the hill
To fetch a pail of water.
Jack fell down *(lower your pitch)* and broke his crown
(touch your head and have a hurt look on your face)
And Jill came tumbling after.

If the author indicates how a character is speaking try to mimic that voice. The child *shouted*, "Leave me alone!"

When you are reading stories like *Three Little Bears*, adopt voices that suit a Mommy, Daddy, or Baby bear. Children really love the baby voice. *Three Billy Goats Gruff* also lends itself to a baby voice and a Mean Old Troll voice. You may find that when reading books like *Franklin* or *Elephant and Piggy*, you adopt a certain voice for these characters. Watch what happens if you forget or change that voice. Your child will tell you, probably very emphatically, that you are not using the correct voice. Add loud, soft, fast, slow, high, low, creepy, excited, or dramatic voices to match the tone and words of the story and you will find not only is your child more engaged but it is also more fun for you.

Reflections on Using Expression

Throughout my career as a teacher, I used expression as a means to engage my readers more deeply with a story. It was fun to mimic a mean troll by using a deep, growly voice; be a baby bear with a high-pitched, squeaky, little voice; or a frightened, anxious child in a trembling, weepy voice.

My students gave me the confidence to become a better oral reader, and I could see their engagement and comprehension had improved. Talking about the emotions and feelings of the characters felt very safe and natural. Sometimes it was a bridge for children to share their feelings and personal experiences and to receive acceptance and empathy from their peers. Using expression helped to make the story come alive and I had so much fun reading aloud. It was a favourite activity for my students and myself. We looked forward to this time every day.

I also learned that enjoying an expressive reader was not exclusive to primary children and with some adaptations, I used this tool no matter what age group I taught. When reading a novel, I would often choose one or two voices for the characters, and that helped the students identify who was speaking. I personally found that I could not have too many different voices, as I would forget which voice went with each character and then it just became confusing!

Reflect to Remember: How to Read with Expression

- Expression increases engagement
- Adopt voices for different characters
- Moderate your voice
- Let your face show emotion

Special Parts of a Book

and Other Things That Merit Attention

We can just open up a book and start reading. It's not that difficult. There are, however, a few things we might do that will really make our reading sessions come alive and be entertaining. (Remember, alive and entertaining equals fun, and fun equals your child wanting to do this activity more and more!) Paying attention to some parts of the book like the title, the first line, the last line and the illustrations will increase your expertise at reading aloud.

The Title

Reading the title of a book is like getting a sniff of something delicious. It holds the promise of wonderful things to come and beckons you to enter. Even authors acknowledge its important. Children's author Eve Bunting wrote:

> Titles are very hard. Sometimes a title comes before I start to write the book, but often I finish the book, and I still don't have a title. I have to go through the book again, and then sometimes I hope a title jumps out at me from what I've written.

Take time with the front cover. Read the title and wonder aloud, "What do you think this book is about?" Look carefully at the cover illustrations and think about what is to come. This helps to prepare your child for the story. It activates and focusses their brain. If you just open the book and start to read you will have missed the opportunity to prepare for what is to come and your child will be playing catch up for a couple of pages.

Even if you have read the book a zillion times, read the title. You may not do the same wondering as the first time but it will help to activate the brain. Authors agonize over the crafting the perfect title, one which can captivate in just a few words and entice the reader to read more. The least we can do is read it.

The First Sentence

Reading the first sentence (or sentences) of a story is to start a journey and needs special attention. Read slowly, pause, think, and wonder, then read on. Give your child a moment to enter this world and prepare for what may come. Even if it is an old favourite, you can pretend to forget what happens and say, "Is this the one where the elephant goes across the troll's bridge?" It will delight your child to correct you.

When reading a chapter book, it is tempting to start reading where you have bookmarked your last session. However, it really helps to jog the memory of your audience by reading the last few sentences of the previous chapter or paragraph. (Think about that novel you are reading. Do you always remember what was happening or do you read back a few sentences?)

The Last Sentence

You know you have read a good book when you turn the last page and feel a little as if you have lost a friend.

Paul Sweeney

As you approach the end of a wonderful storybook or novel, it is important to read those last few words slowly, with deliberate pauses, sighs, and reluctance. We are, after all, parting from something we enjoyed and relished. Just like a tender parting at an airport, we reluctantly leave the treasured confines of a book.

Consider the last few lines of *Charlotte's Web* by E. B. White:

> Wilbur never forgot Charlotte. Although he loved her children and grandchildren dearly, none of the new spiders ever quite took her place in his heart. She was in a class by herself. It is not often that someone comes along who is a true friend and a good writer. Charlotte was both.

These lines are begging us to read slowly, gently, and with love. Eye contact and maybe a little snuggle will increase the power of these words and create a connection for this book that will never be lost. Gently close the book and breathe deeply.

Some final lines are not really that well written but you can increase their power if you read slowly and expressively. Even a last line like, "and they all lived happily ever after" can be delivered effectively if you slow down and emphasize the words *all* and *happily*. Make sure to add eye contact and maybe even a contented sigh.

Illustrations

> *Illustrations have as much to say as the text.*
>
> Maurice Sendak

A child's first introduction to art will likely be through the pictures of a book. They will learn to appreciate the beauty of art and often try to create their own interpretations of the words with their crayons.

Pictures also serve a purpose to expand and reveal what a children's author is not able to describe using limited text. The setting, time, and place may all be illustrated on a single page enabling the child to quickly grasp a greater comprehension of the story. In a similar way, characters can be shown in great detail through an illustration rather than a long, descriptive paragraph. In essence, what is not revealed in words can be revealed through an illustration and greatly contribute to a child's understanding of the story.

Children love to pour over illustrations and become more engaged in the story through images. They provide a vehicle for conversation and delight. Children can begin to pretend-read storybooks on their own by turning the pages and "reading" the picture.

Early picture books are a child's first lessons in visual literacy. Today, so much of our media is visual, and it is increasingly important for children to be savvy in interpreting and creating visual images. Take your time and really look at the pictures. Help your child to think about an illustrator's use of colour, size or shapes. Ask questions like, "Why do you think that picture is black and white except for that red car in the middle?" or "Why do you think all the people in this picture look happy?" or "How does the illustrator make the people look happy?" or "What really grabs your attention in this picture?" or "How do you feel when you look at this picture?" The pictures should not be viewed passively because truly, a picture is worth a thousand words! Most of our world is interpreted through our visual sense and our children need to learn to read and make sense of pictures.

Henry David Thoreau offered us some words of wisdom when he said, "The question is not what you look at, but what you see."

Reflect to Remember: Special Parts of the Book

- Read the title and wonder aloud
- Read the first and the last sentences slowly
- Spend time with illustrations

Enhancing the Read-Aloud: Repeat and Talk

Repetition is the mother of learning, the father of action, which makes it the architect of accomplishment.

Zig Ziglar

Repetition and talking while you are reading are two other areas to think about as a read-aloud caregiver. You are probably already doing this when you read, and if not, these ideas will help you enrich your read-aloud.

Repeat

One of the best ways we learn is through repetition. It is so important that developmental molecular biologist John Medina listed two of his twelve rules for learning around repetition: Repeat to Remember, and Remember to Repeat. Fortunately, young children love hearing the same story over and over again. New vocabulary words, ideas, and comprehension of a story are greatly enhanced through repeated readings. Your child (that little sponge) will soak up all this information. When a child voices some little bit of knowledge, it can improve their self-confidence and give them a feeling of mastery. A familiar story and characters may also be very comforting.

Notice when they pick old favourites. Is it just for fun, or are they needing a little security? When a child picks the same story over and over, they know what is going to happen, which gives them a sense of comfort and control. There are no surprises, so children will feel calmer and more secure with familiar stories.

> *from* **PAULINE:**
>
> One day, Connor was sick and I couldn't visit him, so I read his favourite truck book to him on video chat. I think I have read that same book about thirty times but I try and read with the same pizazz as the first time. Now he is always asking to phone Nana so I can read him a story. I just love that!

Another advantage for rereading the same book is to allow your child to more deeply understand the story, the words, or discover something they did not learn the first time.

Even though you may want to pull out all your hair when your child requests *Goodnight Moon* for the zillionth time, take a deep breath, and know it is so good for your little one.

All That Chit Chat

Talking your way through a book can greatly enhance the enjoyment and comprehension of the story. When your child is an infant, it may be simply pointing at a picture, making a sound ("cow," "m-o-o-o-o"), or commenting about the pictures.

Author Mem Fox put it this way:

> The fire of literacy is created by the emotional sparks created between a child, a book, and the person reading it. It isn't achieved by the book alone, nor by the child alone, nor by the adult who's reading aloud—it's the relationship winding between all three, bringing them together is easy harmony.

When your child is a little older, you can make your reading time more powerful by asking questions, making little comments, and talking with your child about what they are hearing and seeing. Questions like, "What do you think is going to happen next?" or "Why do you think she did that?" or "What would you do?" can enhance a child's comprehension of a story. It should feel natural, however, not like a quiz.

If the story is a familiar one, your child might like to finish the sentence or say a favourite line. "And the mean old troll lived under the _____" (child fills in with *bridge*) or "And the mean old troll said, ' _____ '" (child fills in with their meanest, toughest voice, "Who's that crossing my bridge?") Allowing your child to contribute to the story makes them feel smart and part of the story. This is a more interactive way to read with your child, but it should never feel like the talk is impeding the enjoyment of the text. Sometimes it feels right just to read the words on the page, especially if you are worn out, pressed for time, or just want your child to wind down and to go to sleep.

Reflect to Remember: Enhancing the Read-aloud

- Repetition is a simple but very powerful tool for learning.
- Talk through a book to get more out of it and increase your child's comprehension

---

ORAL STORYTELLING

We are all storytellers. We all live in a network of stories. There isn't a stronger connection between people than storytelling.

Jimmy Neil Smith

Why include oral storytelling in a book about reading aloud to children? The common thread is simply the story itself. Human beings are hardwired for stories, and oral storytelling was around long before the book.

Since the time of the ancients, humans have been telling stories as a powerful way to teach, entertain, and honor traditions. Indigenous people have a strong oral tradition, where telling stories is a very important way to make sense of the world. Being an indigenous storyteller is an honoured position, and storytellers are trained and given the right to share stories. A common theme in indigenous storytelling concerns the preservation of the land and the animals. Some stories are entertaining or tell about personal, family, or community. Storytelling can offer a shared narrative of a culture, family, or situation. It strengthens the bonds of a family or a community.

Benefits of Oral Storytelling

Storytelling can be used as effectively today as it was thousands of years ago. For children, listening to stories helps with vocabulary, comprehension, and self-regulation, similar to reading a book. Furthermore, the listeners can create their own visuals in their head, which will help prepare them for reading novels or other texts without pictures.

Telling a story is often expressive and told directly to an audience. The eye contact, facial emotions, and gestures offer an intimate connection with the storyteller, and young listeners will often better comprehend an oral story than one that is read. Oral storytelling can be deeply personal and help to create strong bonds between the listener and the storyteller.

The expense or scarcity of books can leave children without an important and fun learning experience, but much of this can be made up simply by an adult telling their own stories. The added bonus is the story within you can be accessed at any time and in any place. Imagine being with an anxious child in a hospital room. Just by sitting close to your child and saying something like, "I want to tell you a story about the first time Mommy was in the hospital." Or, "Did you know you were born in a hospital? It was a day just like this…" In just a few words you will have captured your child's attention and offered a little calm and security. You can turn any situation into an opportunity to tell a story. And if you can't think of a new story, tell an old one.

from MARY M:

After camping for three days, we prepared ourselves for the gruelling thirty-km hike back to the truck. Our boys were teenagers and our youngest, Naomi, was eleven. We had hiked as a family since the kids were little, but this was a big one. We had made it in, so we could make it out. The boys took off ahead of us for the last few kilometres, but my husband, Naomi, and I were exhausted.

The weather was unrelenting rain, the trail was slippery, and our bodies ached. My daughter's feet were sore and blistered, and I could tell she just wanted to give up. We had to keep going. I don't know why I thought to do this but I started to tell the Thunderbird legend, an indigenous story about a creature with extraordinary strength and power. The story is not that long, so I had to really go slow and stretch it out. Amazingly, Naomi became quiet and continued to put one foot in front of the other. Before we knew it, we were back at the truck. We had become so focused on the story that all our aches and pains became secondary.

What Stories To Tell?

You will have heard many stories by the time you are an adult and you can retell those to your child. *Three Little Bears, The Gingerbread Boy, Cinderella,* or *Aladdin* are stories you might remember. You don't have to retell the story exactly as it was told to you. Maybe Goldilocks becomes an African-American little girl named Shonna, or Cinderella decides to strike out on her own, get an education, and become a teacher. Maybe the Gingerbread Boy morphs into an alien that runs away to another galaxy. Your child will probably like your version better, and it will become one of those family traditions that is passed on to the next generation. Tell a story about a movie you saw, a song you heard, or a novel you read.

Some adults do not feel confident in their own literacy skills and are reluctant to read to their children. Some just like to tell stories rather than read them. Memories of that uncle or grandma who used to tell stories and make us laugh gave us comfort and a sense of belonging. There are people who tell stories to teach a lesson. Many of the old legends and myths were lessons passed down to teach future generations right from wrong as well as tell us who we are and where we have come from.

The more stories you tell, the better storyteller you will become. When you add expression, different voices, or moderate your speech in other ways, you will increase the connections with your listeners. Adding gestures will also enhance a story.

from EMILY:

Uncle Kirk was the storyteller in the family, and we all looked forward to his visits. He had a way of drawing you in and mesmerizing you with wild tales of his early life. We would sit around the dinner table for hours and no one would want to leave. We laughed until our sides ached but still begged for more. His stories were a glue that held us together and made us rejoice in being a family. And because I felt this strong connection, he was also someone I trusted to go to for advice.

Elements of a Good Story

Creating a good story basically requires four things:

1. An interesting character with a goal and motive.
2. Obstacles to overcome to achieve a goal.
3. The character struggles. Other characters or resources may help to overcome obstacles.
4. Obstacles are overcome, goal is reached.

Think about the *Three Billy Goats Gruff*.

1. The interesting goal is the green grass on the other side of the bridge. The motive is hunger.

2. The obstacle is the mean old troll living under the bridge.
3. Two billy goats struggle and fail to cross the bridge. Biggest billy goat arrives. (obstacle and struggle)
4. Big billy goat pushes the troll off the bridge (obstacle overcome) and all the goats cross the bridge and eat the grass. (goal achieved)

When Emily was in primary school, we began an imaginative story about Timmy and Sadie, two forest squirrels. Timmy was a blind, gentle, old squirrel who would often be fretting about finding nuts and navigating the forest. His wife was the chubby, lovable, and infinitely patient Sadie. Sadie was devoted to Timmy. Night after night, we would make up a story about their adventures, and some nights we would veer off into wild and unfathomable scenarios that left us roaring with laughter. These stories sometimes grew out of my hesitancy to read the same old books once again, or just to add another adventure for Timmy and Sadie. Once began, they became a favourite that we would go back to again and again.

A fun activity to do with your child to help encourage them to tell their own stories is to take turns retelling a familiar story or making up a new one. The first person begins, then abruptly stops, and the other person continues to tell the story. You continue this way, back and forth. The results can be hilarious.

from CHRIS:

I sometimes make up stories, or Cullen will ask for what he calls, an "imagination" story. Usually, it is about a superhero who faces some of the same problems that Cullen has encountered. It's hard to always think fast as I am making up these stories, and sometimes Cullen will disagree with how the story is evolving so I have to backtrack and retell it so it is "Cullen-approved." He also likes to give me the main characters, say a penguin and batman, and I have to make up the story.

The science of storytelling tells us that whatever is happening in a story is happening to us as well, at a brain level. When our brains are engaged in a story, they stop flitting around in endless daydreams. It is estimated that we engage in thousands of daydreams a day but listening to an engaging story can still our overactive minds and make us pay attention.

In short, humans are hard-wired for stories. They are powerful ways to teach and entertain. If you can't lay your hands on a book or want to vary the enjoyment of a story, be a storyteller.

Reflect to Remember: Oral Storytelling

- Storytelling is a powerful way to teach, entertain and honor traditions
- Personal stories help to "glue" a family together
- Four main requirements for a good story: character, obstacle, struggle, success

RELUCTANT AND STRUGGLING READERS

*If you don't like to read, you haven't found
the right book.*

Maya Angelou

Keeping our children engaged with books can sometimes be challenging. This chapter will discuss some ideas to keep your children involved with books. You will learn about how to encourage the reluctant child, some ideas for struggling readers and children who have disabilities. Although this book is not about teaching your children how to read, I firmly believe if children do not value or find pleasure in books, they will likely have some reading difficulties or lack an important source of intellectual stimulation and knowledge.

Making sure your child stays turned on to books is important at any age, even when they can independently read their own books. Basic functional literacy is equated to about a Grade Eight level. Higher levels of literacy are equated with better health, better jobs, not dropping out of school and staying out of jail.

Reluctant Readers

If parents have been reading aloud since birth, the children are not often reluctant to have a book time. However, as they get older and other activities compete for their time, they may not be as interested. Children who are reluctant to have a regular story time usually fall into three categories:

- They lack motivation
- They have a learning disability
- They lack reading skill

You will hear all kinds of things like, "Stories suck," "I hate books," or "It's boring." So now your job is a little more difficult but not impossible. Reread the opening chapter of this book on the compelling reasons to read aloud. If you are convinced that this is something you feel will enhance your child's life and open doors to so many opportunities, read on.

Over the course of a few days, really observe your child. How do they spend their time? What activities seem to be favourites? How much of their time is spent with devices, including television? It there a quiet time at home when reading could take place? Do you have books in your home? Do you have a comfy place to read?

Quietly check out their hearing and eyesight. If you have any concerns, schedule an appointment with your doctor. If your child has not had an eye exam (about three is the usual age for a first exam), book one and make sure you mention if your child is struggling with learning to read.

During this observational period, also check out how you and your partner spend your time. Do you model reading? If you value reading and books, your child is way more likely to value them as well. Talk with your partner about how, as a family, you could help your child. Be a reader yourself. Preview lots of books, so you might be able to place that just-right book on your child's lap. Lead by example. When you are at the library, choose a few books for yourself and let your child see you reading them. Talk about the book you just read.

Some things to try

If your child is lacking motivation to share books with you, there are several things you might try. You could vary how they read. For instance, they could choose to read independently, listen to an audio book, have you read aloud, or share reading aloud. The object is to keep your kid happily engaged with books. Some children might enjoy a reading challenge: "How many books do you think we could read this month?" Keep a chart so your child can see their progress.

Start by setting up a reading environment in your home. For example, as your child begins to collect a few of their own books, make sure they have a shelf or bookcase to display them. Do they have a comfy chair? Then look around your house. Are there places for books and other reading material?

If your child loves to read aloud, listen. Other alternatives are to share reading pages or chapters. Similar to oral storytelling, you take turns reading the book. You may find that you love listening to your child read and relish this time together. Perhaps your child might enjoy reading to you while you are making dinner or driving.

If your child is really balking at being read to, try reading the same book independently and then having a conversation about the book. However your child chooses to read, try to have conversations about what they are reading and talk about what you are reading as well.

Ask librarians and teachers for help. Look online under subjects such as, "great books for reluctant readers," or "best books for eight-year-olds." Talk with your child's teacher about what books they look at in class, and see if your school library will let you borrow books.

Be honest with your child about why you want to hook them on books. Tell them you will be there for them, and every day an adult will share some book time with them. Decide when and where you will read together. If your child is older, please include them on this decision.

Decide how much time you will dedicate to reading. I recommend starting with just a few minutes, say ten, and as your child gets hooked on books, they will want to spend more time. In fact, they will probably not be concerned at all about the time.

The first time you sit down with your child, you may not read at all. Find out what kind of subjects they like. Do they like humour, sports, adventures, factual information? Suggest a trip to the library, bookstore, or spend some time online at a book site. Self-selection needs to be paramount. The nice thing about a library is that you can choose several books and have the luxury to try a few without putting out any money. Include fiction or non-fiction, graphic novels and comic books, magazines, or whatever seems to appeal to your child.

Think about the magazine. If you are a hunter, car lover, chef, or science enthusiast, remember there are magazines for all these subjects. It is surprising how many magazines there are for young people. Let your child see you reading these magazines and leave them out to be casually picked up. Kids like getting something delivered to the door so what about a monthly subscription for a magazine of their choice? It may sound rather old-fashioned to have physical magazines and books, but I believe their actual presence can motivate a child to pick it up and thumb through it. You can't get that by looking at the outside of a phone or iPad.

You might try to pair reading with something they like. For instance, read a book and then see the movie. Read a recipe book and make some cookies. Read about fishing, get the right gear and go fishing. Read about the stars and visit a planetarium. Read a gardening book, plant a garden (or just one plant!). If it's a novel and the characters are doing something like tracking a bear, go into the woods and try to find animal tracks. If the characters are planning a party, plan a family and friend's party. You get the idea...something you read...something fun to do.

Other ideas are to read a shorter book or at least books with short chapters. Something that doesn't seem too intimidating. If you read a book that is part of a series, you might just hook your child on the whole series. You might try an audio book in the car.

Motivating a reluctant child is not easy, and it will take some effort on your part. The rewards are worth it so I hope you will persevere and maybe your whole household will turn on to reading.

---

from **GRETEL:**

My son Adam was very different than his sister, always wiggling and wanting to move. He did not learn to read early but he did like listening to stories. One of his favourites was *Go Bear Go*, and we read that a lot. Whatever he wanted to listen to, I read. I thought if I could just keep him interested in stories, then eventually he would find a book that was meaningful enough to him and he would want to read. In school he discovered the Goosebumps series, and then he read every one he could lay his hands on. That was the beginning of Adam becoming a reader.

Struggling Readers

Children seem to know when they are not meeting expectations. For many children, the urge to hide this deficit is to pretend to be a reader. I have observed children who have their book boxes ready, are quiet, and take out a book and look like they are engaged in reading. What is their motivation? Why pretend to read? The answer is shame. A feeling of inadequacy. A fear of appearing stupid. It starts as early as Grade One when children begin to notice they are struggling and see their peers choose books and read with seeming ease. Some children memorize text, choose a book that has been read aloud, or one that has been made into a movie. When asked about the book, they can usually answer general questions. So they continue to hide. They are quiet and compliant. They just don't want to be exposed because the shame and humiliation would be unbearable. Most teachers will try and intervene, try to support that child, but the truth is resources and time are always in short supply. By the time these children reach grades three and four, they have mastered pretend reading and are rarely identified for support.

And what might that support be? To remove them from the class for extra instruction? To give them appropriate level reading material? What nine-year-old wants to be singled out or be seen with "a baby book" when his peers are reading Harry Potter? The truth is that there are no easy answers for the child who starts behind and does not receive intensive intervention. They usually stay behind, not because they lack the intellectual capacity but because their opportunities for early stimulation and learning were not met.

If you have a child with a reading disability or they lack some reading skills, they may not be able to read something at their age level, so by continuing to read aloud, you will be honouring and stimulating their intellectual competence. It is also important to know that most children ages six to thirteen have a listening age that is two to three years above their reading age. This means the books they may have difficulty decoding can still be understood in a read-aloud. In fact, these may be the very books they feel are really interesting and engaging. At about eighth grade, their listening and reading ages come into balance.

Unfortunately, some schools insist students only read books at their assessed reading level. This can be a soul-sucker for the child's interests and can also kill the love of reading. Instruction at their reading level is necessary but does not need to include every book they encounter. Just because they bring home a little reading book for home reading, do not assume all other books are off the table. Personal choice should be the mainstay of reading. All the above ideas for motivating your child to engage with books apply to children who are struggling so make it pleasurable.

I recall one of my students, Austin. He idolized the older boys in our multigrade class. He started reading the *Magic Treehouse Series* because the older boys read every book. Then he noticed they went on to the *Hardy Boys*, which was a giant leap in terms of language. Although the older boys were not too challenged, I worried Austin would not meet with the same kind of success. I didn't say anything when he signed the book out and would periodically check in with him about the story. He admitted it was quite hard but he persevered. It took about six months, but he finished the book. His reading improved and when he chose the next *Hardy Boys* book, I was not concerned.

from EMILY

It is difficult to hook struggling readers on books, especially if they think they are "baby" books. One Grade Four student was very reluctant to engage with books until I found a series of high-interest, low-vocabulary books. These books are written for older students, look like novels, and have chapters. Their limited and easily decodable vocabulary really suits the needs of struggling readers. The covers even look cool. My student started to look forward to reading with me and his friends, and I could see his reading and his confidence really improved.

Reflect To Remember:
Reluctant and Struggling Readers

- Engaging the reluctant reader will require some out-of-the-box thinking and commitment
- Think about what your child enjoys; try to capitalize on these things
- Start small; gradually increase time spent with books
- Reflect on how your family currently spends their time

TECHNOLOGY

I say tech is like fire. If you don't know how to use it, you will burn the house down. If you do know how to use it, it will advance us as a civilization.

Dr. Shimi Kang

Our world has made dramatic changes in the past few decades because of advancements in technology, particularly personal devices. The past decade has changed the landscape for what children are doing, and we are learning the hard way that much of it, especially for young children, is not good.

Even my dog seems to know that when I am on my phone, I am not available for her. She will go to her toy box and try to entice me with a toy. If I do not respond, she eventually goes to her bed, and with a heavy sigh, lays down. I think if she were still a puppy, she would not give up so easily but probably start racing around or tearing things apart. I see children desperate for their parents' attention, and sometimes they just quietly give up but other times they throw tantrums. Our basic human need is to connect with others, and our digital devices are blocking that far too often.

On the other hand, these devices are the tools we use to navigate our world and have made so many things better. Information at our fingertips, contacts with friends and loved ones, and entertainment a click away, to name just a few advantages. We are the guinea pigs in this huge technological leap, and how we use it can be wonderful or devastating.

These devices are expensive, but oh, so cool, so desired, so attainable, so addicting. They hit the markets before we had the time to carefully examine or study their effects. They come with no warnings or advice. Now they are here, they are not going away, and we must learn to use these tools to our and our children's best advantage.

Guidelines for Usage

As adults, we know that what is good for us is not necessarily good for children. We have rules about when you can drive, when you can vote, when you can drink alcohol, or when you can work. Something as powerful as our little devices comes with no rules. The American Academy of Child and Adolescent Psychiatry (Feb. 2020) and similar organizations around the globe, issued guidelines for children and technology:

Birth to 18 months: none (except video conferencing with an adult)
2-5 years old: one hour a day accompanied by an adult
Older children /adults: Two hours a day of recreational screen time

If our children exceed these guidelines, it can be arduous to try and rein them in, so it is in their best interests to apply some rules. We now know there are many negative effects that too much screen time may have on our children. The global pandemic has also had a huge impact on the amount of time our children are using screens. Watching our children slip into this digital abyss can seem overwhelming.

from PATRICIA:

I have observed parents and children on planes, and how parents will help their children pass the time. The two activities most often chosen are reading books or playing on an electronic device. The children who are reading seem calmer, more engaged, less wiggly and happier. Those who have devices do not seem calm or particularly happy. Although they are sitting close to a mother or father, they seem so disconnected. It's kind of sad.

The more time a child spends in a virtual world, the less time they are playing, moving, exploring, or interacting with friends and family—the very things that make a healthy child. Too much screen time can have a profound effect on brain development and social and emotional growth. Developmental delays and deficits that are avoidable are actually becoming more commonplace and noted when children enter primary school. Professors have noticed changes in young people entering college as well. This is preventable. As parents and caregivers, we must tame this giant that lurks in our homes and at our fingertips.

If the guidelines seem severe or restrictive compared to what you are presently doing, keep in mind that it is a guideline and try to make it a goal. Don't beat yourself up when it doesn't happen. Always have these guidelines in the back of your mind and keep trying. Aim for better, not perfect.

Setting Healthy Limits

Many parents use devices as a calming tool or babysitter. While this is understandable, and there are times when you are so grateful to have a few quiet minutes, make a point to do it infrequently. It is also important children learn to self-regulate emotions, such as boredom, tantrums, or not getting what they want. You are there to help them through. Parents should also ask caregivers about the possible use of technology and what kind—movies? games?—and how long? You have every right to set limits for your child.

It is easier to limit excess use of technology if your child has learned to enjoy:

- Playing with other children
- Playing or creating by themselves
- Listening to stories and talking with others
- Self-regulating with books, music or quiet time

These activities, done from birth, are what they need for optimal development.

Make a Family Plan

Limiting screen time is not only a problem for children but may also be a problem for parents. What you model, your child will emulate. So before applying restrictions for your children, check your own usage. Using technology in your home should be a plan for everyone. Parents are advised, especially for children under five, to use devices *with* your child. Be aware of what they are watching, what their interests are and use the devices to enhance your relationship, not cause a separation.

Find a way to include your family values with technology. For instance, if your family values creating fun crafts from nature, spend time with your child looking for ideas on Pinterest or other crafting sites. If you love science experiments, try researching ideas together. If you want to share your love of digital storytelling, create stories with your children. In other words, make technology an extension of your interests and your child's interests.

---

from CATHERINE:

We don't have a lot of technology for our kids—no iPads or phones or DVD player in the car. The kids always have to ask before they turn on the TV. When we are driving, I tell them to look out the window at this beautiful world we live in. At the cabin there is a TV for DVDs but the rule is we can't use it unless it is raining.

You Are Not Alone

We know our children's future is a digital one and we want to make sure they are prepared for that as well. All screen time is not the same. As much as possible, be a part of your child's digital world and recognize you are not alone in facing challenges around technology.

Some parents will need help managing technology usage in their homes. Many feel ashamed, absolutely overwhelmed, and do not know where to turn to for help. Begin a conversation about technology usage with your doctor, health nurse, or your child's teacher. Maybe it could be a focus for your parent group at school. It's easier to set guidelines when you know you are not alone.

from **KRISTA:**

My daughter was invited to a birthday lunch at a restaurant with her friend. As soon as we were seated, the other mom gave her children tablets. My children don't have any devices. There they sat, all dressed up for a party, and there were no conversations between the children. It was really sad.

from **ANNA:**

I think it is important to read to your kids even in the face of technology. It gives me individual time with each child, and they feel comfortable, safe and calmer. I have seen the benefits. It's not always easy. There can be lots of tears and tantrums.

from **KATIE:**

My son is in middle school now, and he doesn't have a phone. We talk about it from time to time, and he will eventually have one. But right now, he hangs out with his friends and loves to bike all over the place. Fortunately, his friend's parents think the same way I do and have made strong commitments to limit technology.

Printed Book or E-Book?

Another question that may arise around the use of our devices is, "What is the best way to read? Through a device or a book?" At the present time there is evidence that book/paper learning offers some benefits that screens do not. Reading a book makes it easier for parents and children to control their interactions with the text.

They can decide what words need explaining or repeating, what pictures are worth a deeper look, or what to discuss. Many apps and e-books have too many digital distractions and control how a story is paced. Parent-child interactions with a digital story tend to be more about the mechanics of how to turn a page, moderate the sound, or move an object. Print book interactions are more about the story or our reactions to the story. Using e-books once in a while with older children may add some novelty if you remember to make personal engagement a priority. For young children, the simple print storybook is better for early brain development and emotional connection.

Reflect to Remember: Technology

- Follow guidelines as best you can
- Be a good model for using devices
- Be selective and diligent
- Be an advocate and support other parents; be open with your struggles—you are not alone

BARRIERS AND SOLUTIONS

*Access to books and the encouragement of the
habit of reading: these two things are the first
and most necessary steps in education and
librarians, teachers, and parents all over the
world know it. It is our children's right, and
it is also our best hope and their best hope for
the future.*

Michael Morpurgo

**Every child deserves to be read to on a
regular basis.**

Every child should have access to books.

**Every parent needs access to books,
support, and encouragement to read to
their children.**

Reading is a great equalizer that diminishes the
differences and distances between us. When we read the
same book and have an opportunity to talk about it, we
are on a level playing field. We have the same information

and talking about how we interpret that information can be enlightening in so many ways.

Reading is a form of thinking, and thinking about a book continues long after the final page is read. The information and images we receive from a book can ignite our imagination and stir our souls to consider or reconsider previously held beliefs. Critical thinking, the ability to think deeply about a topic, is triggered through reading. Reading can increase our understanding, move us to empathy and compassion, and be a change agent.

The research is clear. Reading aloud to children makes a huge difference academically, emotionally, and socially. We need to ensure that all families have equal opportunities to make this happen. Parents need support, which must come in many forms.

For many families, it is not enough to give the information on how or why one should read aloud to children. Some have huge struggles and obstacles to overcome before they can begin to think about acquiring books and reading to their children. Poverty, trauma, illness, and war are just some of the reasons why parents are not reading to their children. When we become a society that really loves and honors our children enough to give *all* children equal opportunities, we will see all parents actively and joyfully reading and engaging with their little ones. Below are some political, local, school, and other initiatives to make this a reality. Is there something on the list you can do?

Political Initiatives

- No tax on children's books and or tax credits for children's books
- Living wages so parents don't have to work two or three jobs
- Paid parental leave for all parents
- Quality, affordable daycare
- Affordable medical support
- Literacy agencies to help with low literacy
- In poorer areas or areas not serviced by libraries, deliver books free of charge
- Get all ministerial and support agencies to get the word out about reading to children and regardless of income, provide parental support, mini-libraries and access to books

Local Initiatives

- Get groups like Rotary to donate to libraries
- Get social agencies to provide books for all children on a regular basis.
- Explore Imagination Library as a possibility in your area
- Encourage a "How to Read to Your Child" Q&A event
- Use social media to encourage reading to children

School and Library Initiatives

- Make reading aloud part of all daycare centres, preschools, elementary and secondary schools

- Fund libraries to include book loss as part of operating expenses and as a contribution to getting books for all children
- Advocate for all school and classroom libraries, regardless of where they are located, to have diverse, quality collections that include print and digital media

from LUCI:

Our school offers a summer reading program that is open to all students. All they have to do is talk with our librarian, and they can take home a bag of books for the summer. Most of the books are returned. Our district recognizes there will be book loss and has set up a fund to replace lost books.

Personal Initiatives

- Support low-literacy parents in a non-judgmental, compassionate way and encourage parents to support each other
- Support parents with challenging children
- Encourage grandparents to read aloud

- Encourage many people to give the same message —read to your kids!
- Honor women and mothers and the job they do; support mother's groups and moms helping moms
- Have more than one adult who can read to a child

from MARJORIE:

Parents are busy with work, exhausted, and involved in too many activities. They are often embarrassed or feel guilty about not reading to their children. Sometimes their own low-literacy skills prevent them from reading aloud. I think it is important to share our literacy struggles and I try to help parents find ways to connect with their children.

Reflect To Remember:
Barriers and Solutions

- Some people face huge struggles and are unable to read to their children
- There are ways to help either through political initiatives, getting involved locally, or personally making a difference in someone's life

THE DREAM

*A writer only begins a book. A reader
finishes it.*

Samuel Johnson

My dream for you, dear reader, is a lifetime of
sharing books. Reading to your children, grandchildren,
and maybe even the kid across the street. We need to slow
down, enjoy and learn what the written word has to offer,
and take the time to process these thoughts. In a world of
faster and more, we need our books as well as the
opportunity to be cocooned with a story and a loved one.
We need to talk about what we learn and experience in
calm conversations that make us think, "Well, I never
thought of it that way," or "My, that is interesting," or
"Gee, that is hilarious." It all begins with reading aloud
and sharing stories with our babies.

Every parent wants good things for their children.
Good things are mommy's hugs and daddy's singing and
grandma's cookies and going for a walk with granddad
and playing with siblings and friends. Good things are
finding a treasury of books in all homes and being able to

grab a book and say, "Let's read a story." Good things are seeing your child light up when you read together. Good things are opportunities to read, and the joy and pleasure that comes from sharing a good book. Good things are seeing your child grow and develop an understanding of the world. Good things are seeing the confidence and readiness your child will have to enter that world on their own. We all want good things for our children and sharing books can be a powerful activity to help make that happen.

So, dear reader, what will you read today?

APPENDIX I: BOOK SUGGESTIONS

(Hint: any authors listed here are a good place to search for your next book)

Birth to One

Time for Bed by Mem Fox, illustrated by Jane Dyer

Goodnight Moon by Margaret Wise Brown, illustrated by Clement Hurd

Guess How Much I Love You by Sam Mc Bratney, illustrated by Anita Jeram

Good Morning World by Paul Windsor

Whoever You Are by Mem Fox, illustrated by Leslie Staub

Please, please, baby by Spike Lee and Tonya Lewis Lee, illustrated by Kadir Nelson

Sweetest Kulu by Celina Kalluk, illustrated by Alexandria Neonakis

Goodnight, Goodnight Construction Site by Sherri Daskey Rinker, illustrated by Tom Lichtenheld

Everywhere Babies by Susan Meyers, illustrated by Marla Frazer

A Good Day by Kevin Henkes

Brown Sugar Baby by Kevin Lewis, illustrated by Jestina Southerland

One to Two

Ten Little Fingers and Ten Little Toes by Mem Fox, illustrated by Helen Oxenbury

Hop on Pop by Dr. Seuss

Peek-a WHO? by Nina Laden

Where is Baby's Belly Button by Karen Katz
No David by David Shannon
Brown Bear, Brown Bear, What Do You See? By Bill Martin
    Jr. and Eric Carle
100 First Animals by Caterpillar Books
Bedtime for Sweet Creatures by Nikki Grimes, illustrated
    by Elizabeth Zunon
Love You Head to Toe by Ashley Barron

Two To Three

Hand, Hand, Fingers, Thumb by Al Perkins, illustrated by
    Eric Gurney
I Like Myself by Karen Beaumont, illustrated by David
    Catrow
I Love You Stinky Face by Lisa McCourt
I Am So Mad by Mercer Mayer
If You Give A Mouse A Cookie by Laura Joffe Numeroff,
    illustrated by Felicia Bond
Knuffle Bunny by Mo Willems
Pete the Cat and His Four Groovy Buttons by James Dean,
    illustrated by Eric Litwin
The Very Cranky Bear by. Nick Bland
What Color is Your Underwear? by Sam Lloyd
Baby Bear by Kadir Nelson
Little Blue Truck by Alice Schertle, illustrated by Jill
    McElmurry
Please, Puppy, Please by Spike Lee and Tonya Lewis Lee,
    illustrated by Kadir Nelson

Four To Six

Ish by Peter Reynolds

It's Okay To Be Different by Todd Parr

Olivia by Ian Falconer

The Book With No Pictures by B.J. Novak

There Was An Old Lady Who Swallowed A Fly by Lucille Colandro

Waiting is Not Easy! by Mo Willems

Fancy Nancy by Jane O'Connor, illustrated by Robin Preiss Glasser

Where The Wild Things Are by Maurice Sendak

If I Built A House by Chris Van Dusen

It's Not a Box by Antoinette Portis

Press Here by Herve Tullet

The Day The Crayons Quit by Drew Daywalt, illustrated by Liver Jeffers

Scaredy Squirrel by Melanie Watt

Hair Love by Matthew A. Cherry, illustrated by Vashti Harrison

Daddy Speaks Love by Leah Henderson, illustrated by E.B. Lewis

Tar Beach by Faith Ringgold

Shi-shi-etko by Nicola I. Campbell, illustrated by Kim LaFave

First Novels

Fantastic Mr. Fox by Roald Dahl

Mercy Watson Series by Kate DiCamillo, illustrated by Chris Van Dusen

Dragons and Marshmallows by Asia Citro, illustrated by Marion Lindsay

Baby Monkey, Private Eye by Brian Selznick and David Serlin

Bad Guys by Aaron Blabey

Inside Out and Back Again by Thanna Lai

Six To Eight

Picture Books

Diary of a Fly by Doreen Cronin, pictures by Harry Bliss

17 Things I'm Not Allowed to Do Anymore by Jenny Offill, illustrated by Nancy Carpenter

Interrupting Chicken by David Ezra Stein

How The Raven Stole the Sun by Maria Williams, illustrated by Felix Vigil

The Proudest Blue by Ibtihaj Muhammad, illustrated by Hatem Aly

Thank You, Omu by Oge Mora

The Crossover by Kwame Alexander

Novels

Charlotte's Web by E.B. White, pictures by Garth Williams

Matilda by Roald Dahl, illustrated by Quinten Blake

Ramona the Pest by Beverly Cleary

The Mouse and the Motorcycle by Beverly Cleary

The One and Only Ivan by Katherine Applegate

Captain Underpants by Dav Pilkey

The Lion, The Witch, and The Wardrobe by C.S. Lewis

Inkheart by Cornelia Funke

Diary of a Wimpy Kid by Jeff Kinney
Harry Potter and the Philosopher's Stone by J.K. Rowling
The Barren Grounds by David A. Robertson
Walking in Two Worlds by Wab Kinew

Eight to Ten

The Tale of Desperaux by Kate DiCamillo, illustrated by
    Timothy Basil Ering
Because of Winn Dixie by Kate DiCamillo
Cool by Michael Morpurgo
Magic School Bus Series
Amazing Days of Abby Hayes by Anne Mazer
Geronimo Stilton Series by Geronimo Stilton
Peter and the Star Catchers by Dave Barry and Ridley
    Pearson
How to Train Your Dragon by Cressida Cowell
O*ne Dog and His Boy* by Eva Ibbotson
Harry Potter Series by J.K. Rowling
The Christmas Pig by J.K. Rowling
A Series of Unfortunate Events: The Bad Beginning by
    Lemony Snicket
The Graveyard Book by Neil Gaiman
Alex Rider Stormbreaker by Anthony Horowitz
Pax by Sara Pennypacker
Doll Bones by Holly Black
Bud, Not Buddy by Christopher Paul Curtis

Ten to Twelve

*The Lightning Thief: Percy Jackson and the Olympians, Book
    1* by Rick Riordan

The Hobbit by J.R.R. Tolkien
New Kid by Jerry Craft
Linked by Gordon Korman
Eragon by Christopher Paolini
The Girl Who Drank the Moon by Kelly Barnhill
The Golden Compass Series by Philip Pullman
The Phantom Tollbooth by Norton Juster
Because of Mr. Terupt by Rob Buyea
Touching Spirit Bear by Ben Mikaelsen
Daughter of the Deep by Rick Riordan
Bloom by Kenneth Oppel
Hatchet by Gary Paulsen
A Long Walk to Water by Linda Sue Park
Counting by 7s by Holly Goldberg Sloan
Out of My Mind by Sharon Draper
The Good Turn by Sharna Jackson
Fatty Legs by Christy Jordan-Fenton and Margaret Pokiak-Fenton

Graphic Novels

Amulet series by Kazu Kibuishi
Dog Man series by Dav Pilkey
Bone series by Jeff Smith
New Kid by Jerry Craft
Babymouse series by Jennifer L. Holm, illustrated by Matthew Holm
Cat Kid Comic Club series by Dav Pilkey
Minecraft by R Ste Monster
Smile by Raina Telgemeier
Sonic The Hedgehog by Ian Flynn

The Hilda Troll series by Luke Pearson
Zita the Spacegirl Trilogy by Ben Hatke
Hilo, The Boy Who Crashed to Earth by Judd Winick
Owly series by Andy Runton

Notable Non-Fiction

Martin's Big Words: The Life of Dr. Martin Luther King, Jr. by Doreen Rappaport
Turtle Island The Story of North America's First People by Eldon Yellowhorn and Kathy Lowinger
Snowflake Bentley by Jacqueline Briggs Martin
Apex Predators: The World's Deadliest Hunters, Past and Present by Steve Jenkins
Counting On Snow by Maxwell Newhouse
I Am Jane Goodall: Ordinary People Change the World by Brad Meltzer
DK Eyewitness Books Series by Juliette Clutton-Brock
The Way Things Work by David Macaulay
The Scoop on Poop by Wayne Lynch
Honeybee: The Busy Life of Apis Mellifera by Candace Fleming
Lift the Flap Questions and Answers About Your Body by Katie Dayne, Illustrated by Marie-Eve Tremblay
Alpha Bravo Charlie: The Complete Book of Nautical Codes by Sara Gillingham
Pride: Celebrating Diversity & Community by Robin Stevenson
13½ Incredible Things You Need To Know About Everything DK Publishing

Speaking Our Truth: A Journey of Reconciliation by
Monique Gray Smith
The Arrival by Shaun Tan
Ghost Train by Paul Yee

Humour

0-3

A Little Stuck by Oliver Jeffers
Grumpy Monkey by Suzanne Lang
Sheep In A Jeep by Nancy E. Shaw
No David by David Shannon
Look by Jeff Mack
Toot by Leslie Patricelli

4-6

Don't Let The Pigeon Drive the Bus by Mo Willems
The Twits by Roald Dahl
The Wonky Donkey by Craig Smith
Spoon by Amy Krouse Rosenthal
I Have to Go! By Robert Munsch
Two Dogs by Ian Falconer
Click, Clack, Moo: Cows That Type by Doreen Cronin

6-8

Captain Underpants Series by Dav Pilkey
Bad Guy Series by Aaron Blabey
The Adventures of Nanny Piggins by R.A. Spratt
How to Eat Fried Worms by Thomas Rockwell
Ivy and Bean by Annie Barrows

Dory Fantasmagory by Abby Hanlon
Amelia Bedelia Series by Peggy Parish
Mercy Watson to the Rescue by Kate DiCamillo

9-12

Diary of a Wimpy Kid by Jeff Kinney
Tales of a Fourth Grade Nothing by Judy Blume
The Puffin Book of Funny Stories
The Terrible Two by Jory John and Mac Barnett
The Quickwick Papers Series by Tom Angleberger
Al Capone Does My Shirts by Gennifer Choldenko
Sideways Stories From Wayside School by Louis Sachar
Pippi Longstocking by Asterid Lindgren
The Stinky Cheese Man and Other Fairly Stupid Tales by
    Jon Scieszka and Lane Smith
The Vicar of Nibbleswicke by Roald Dahl

Appendix II: Concepts of Print

Concepts of print are prerequisite skills to reading. Basically, to become a reader, you will have to know how a book is structured and basic components that make up language. This is a learned skill. Not all cultures have the same rules—some books may be structured from back to front and read bottom to top, right to left.

Some of the concepts of print for the English language are:

1. **How to hold a book**. (Just try giving your child a book upside down and watch them turn it the right way around.)

2. **Where to begin a book.** (Give your child a book with the last cover facing them and see if they turn the book around)

3. **The Title.** When you are reading to a child use the words, "The title of this book is…." Run your finger under the title and soon your child will understand this term.

4. **Letters**. Draw your child's attention to a word that begins with the same letter as their name. "Look, that word begins with the same letter as your name." Another time you might say, "That letter begins with Daddy's name," or "Look how big the author made those letters," or "Can you find a letter like this one?" Your child may or may not show a bigger interest in letters but take the cue from them and don't force it. You are not trying to teach the names of the letters;

you are just helping your child recognize what is a letter.

5. **Words.** Draw your child's attention to a word by saying something like, "That's a funny word," or "That sure is a long word." Run your finger under it and say it again. Count the number of words on a page. You are not trying to teach your child to read words, you are just helping your child recognize what is a word.

6. **Sentences.** Draw your child's attention to a sentence by running your finger under a sentence as you read it and say something like, "Boy that is a long sentence," and read it again. Or "I wonder why the author repeats that sentence again and again?" You are teaching your child the meaning of the term *sentence.*

7. **Spaces.** This may seem obvious but children need to recognize that there are spaces between sentences and words for a reason. It is fun to imagine with your child what it would be like if there were no spaces. Read aloud a few lines or even a couple of words all jammed together. Don't be afraid to exaggerate a little and make it really funny.

8. **Where to start reading.** With your finger under the words, start at the top and move to the bottom. Sweep your finger under the sentences, going left to right, then do a return sweep to the left again. Again, this may seem really obvious to you but not all languages are constructed in a top-to-bottom, left-to-right way. This is something we learn.

9. **Punctuation.** Draw your child's attention to the little dot at the end of a sentence. Say, "This is called a period." Tell them that means to stop and then go on to the next sentence. Ask them to imagine if there were no periods and read a passage without stopping and exaggerate being all out of breath at the end. Don't forget to use the term *period* again and again.

10. **Upper and Lower Case letters.** Draw your child's attention to the letter at the beginning of a sentence and say, "This is called an *upper case* letter. Notice how it is different from the other letters. The other letters are called *lower case* letters." Hunt for capital letters. Hunt for lower case letters.

You may be thinking, "These are so easy; of course, my child knows this." It is hard to wrap your head around something that you may have internalized so well with something your child has to learn. Put yourself in your child's shoes and try to read the following lines below:

Can you decode this message?

⅂↔◀↓↙   ◢↕▶   ↗↔↕▷   ◀↑⇨   △▶↙⇨▽⅃
↓◀'▽   ⇨↙↙   ↖▶▽◀   ⇨   ⇨↕⇦⇨↘

Hints:
The message is written top to bottom, left to right, the same as English.

a = ⇨	j = ↖	s = ▽
c = ⇨	l = ↙	t = ◀
d = ⇦	n = ↔	u = ▶
e = ⇨	o = ↕	, = ⊥
i = ↓	r = △	

Did you get it? Or do you need some hints? The message translates as: "Until you know the rules, it's all just a code!" Now think of a child entering Kindergarten not knowing how a book works. It will take time and may seem rather dry and pointless.

If this "learning" starts to feel like formal teaching instead of five-seconds observations, you are overdoing it. If you read to your child every day, you will have hundreds of opportunities to model the concepts of print. If you use the correct terms like *word, sentence, front, back, upper case, period, title,* and *author* over and over again, your child will quietly absorb this knowledge. If they can remember that Tyrannosaurus Rex lived 63 million years ago during the Cretaceous period, they can handle little words like *upper case* and *lower case*! Please use correct terminology.

Some children will *want* to go further. They will *want* to learn the names of the letters and spell words. Some children just seem to take to reading with little difficulty and love the challenge. If that happens it's great, but don't worry if it doesn't. Your job is simply to read every day to your child. The rest will happen at school.

Always read joyously and without an overt academic agenda. Trust that your child is learning.

ABOUT THE AUTHOR

Mary Kretlow has read thousands of children's books throughout her career as a teacher and thousands more as a mother. She taught all the elementary grades and even spent a few years as a teacher librarian. Needless to say, books are a passion. Currently she is a board member for a local literacy foundation and volunteers for "Fostering Literacy" by reading aloud in schools. She knows the power and pleasure of sharing a book and wants all children to have these wonderful experiences. When she's not reading or writing about reading, she can be found carving nature trails through the forest, walking her dog, tending her gardens, hanging out with family and friends, or sipping tea by the river.